# Live Move Be

*An Ex-Evangelical's Journey from*
*Fundamentalism to Freedom*

BRIAN WHITE

The stories in this book reflect the author's recollection of events, bolstered by saved email correspondence and journal entries. Some names and identifying details have been changed to protect the privacy of individuals and organizations.

Cover photo by Kelly Sikkema on Unsplash

# CONTENTS

# FOREWORD

I can remember waking up from a deep sleep when I was eight years old, scared that I was going to hell. The next week I was baptized and for the next 35 plus years, I was filled with constant doubt about whether I had checked all the boxes to be on the good side. If you have lived your life with doubts, fear, anxiety or questions about God, heaven, hell, and Christianity, then you need to read this book.

This is a book that provides real hope to people that are struggling, asking questions, afraid of asking questions, and how all of that pertains to their faith and their future. One of the challenges of being a Christian – at least a conservative evangelical one like I was – is that if you have questions or doubts then you are exposing yourself as not having faith or not willing to accept things in faith.

I got to know Brian when I began attending his church Ekklesia eight years ago. He has since become one of my best friends, and has had a huge influence on me and my faith. His story has inspired me to ask the tough questions, and has given me the strength and courage to face my fears and pull that thread on the sweater knowing full well I would never be able to put it back together. This direct view into his personal journey provides real insight into the questions many of us have about God and eternity.

Reading or not reading this book is much like the decision of taking the "Red Pill" or the "Blue Pill" from the movie *The Matrix*. Reading this book is deciding to take the "Red Pill," which is the pill of brutal truth and reality, but which ultimately leads to freedom. Not reading it is a choice to accept the "Blue Pill," which keeps you in the status quo and security of blissful ignorance.

John 8:32 says "you shall know the truth and the truth shall set you free." If you already feel truly free, then take the "Blue Pill." But if you feel doubt, fear, insecurity or just have questions and want the truth, I challenge you to dive in to this "Red Pill" book and see where the rabbit hole leads. You might find what I found: peace.

Wally Olson

# PREFACE

Let's get this out of the way at the very beginning – I wrote this primarily for me.

It's not that I don't care about you and what you think. On the contrary, interactions with some of you who are reading this provided significant impetus in moving this from a vague idea to an actual product. But you are not the primary reason for what you're reading. The primary reason for this writing is because I feel some need to document just exactly what has happened to me since 2004, and historically, I process things best by writing about them. You see, I've undergone some big changes in my faith over these past 15 years – changes that I didn't order but couldn't have prevented any more than I could prevent the sun from rising tomorrow.

To some of you who know me, the fact that I have undergone a significant evolution in my faith may be news, but it's not something you get to in small talk or in surface level "catching up." And, I have had a hard time understanding the change myself, let alone articulating it. So, if you know me but weren't aware of the change – or perhaps you knew about it, but weren't aware of the extent of it – I hope you don't feel bad about that. I didn't intentionally exclude you (well, maybe some of you). Mostly I just didn't know how to talk about it. Many of you will understand that better as you read this.

However, some of you reading this have been in close proximity to me during at least some part of this journey. Some of you may be confused by what has happened to me. You don't know exactly what happened, why it happened, and might be very concerned that it did happen. That's understandable. When I first began writing this, I was still very much trying to figure it out myself.

I grew up in a moderate small-town Methodist home and church, but converted to different version of the Christian faith in my late teens: *conservative evangelical Christianity*. Now I wouldn't have said I was converting to conservative evangelical Christianity; I was simply becoming a Christian, period. And generally speaking, most conservative evangelical Christians don't think of themselves as conservative evangelicals per se; they think of themselves as simply Christians. Maybe they'll add something like *conservative* or *Bible-believing* as a qualifier, but by and large, they don't go around identifying themselves by the name *conservative evangelical*.

But that name is commonly used to describe a version of Christianity that embraces the Bible as God's definitive and infallible message for humanity, and accepts its contents as being literally true without question; believes Jesus Christ's substitutionary death on the cross paid the penalty for the sins of humanity, and; each person must individually believe in Jesus and accept that payment for yourself in order to gain a place in heaven and avoid an eternity in hell. I will use *conservative evangelical* throughout this book as a shorthand to describe that kind of Christian faith.

This is the version of Christianity that I embraced for over 25 years, and if you knew me earlier in my adult life, you would have known me as a committed adherent. However, the shift over the past 15 years is simply this: I have evolved from a conservative evangelical Christian to something else; something decidedly not conservative or evangelical, which would have been simply inconceivable to me earlier in my adult life.

I am by no means alone. Millions and millions of people of faith – past and present – have experienced or are experiencing something similar to what I have. I know from experience: it is lonely, and you feel like you're losing your mind, your moorings, your community, your friends, and your faith. By writing this, I hope to shed light on a part of the spiritual journey that is often not talked about, not well understood, and in many cases, feared and avoided at all costs.

When I first began writing this, the initial idea was to write something to my former conservative evangelical tribe to explain what had happened to me. In March 2009, a couple that my wife Michelle and I were close to when we lived in Dallas visited us for a couple of days with their children. After their visit, I wrote this in my journal:

> It was great seeing and spending some time with them again. But, as is now typical when I spend time with people I was close to in my former conservative Christian life, there are some awkward moments for me, and I come away somewhat exhausted and feeling like I was a bit fake for not fully owning

up to where I am now theologically. Michelle thinks that's the way it should be; no need to say things that will drive a wedge between us given that we only see one another for a few days every few years. That might be true for now, but is that the way it should be forever? At some point, in order to really be friends, don't I have to come clean to them, at the risk of them rejecting me at worst, or more likely, just thinking I've gone off the deep end and am now a heretic, apostate, and essentially a non-Christian? I don't know, but I will feel this tension every time I spend time with old friends. I felt it this summer when we spent time with old friends from Wichita. Experiencing this again has made me feel a bit depressed, confused and alone.

I've thought about writing something that is addressed to those who knew me in my former life, and explains on some level what I've been through and where I am now. Would this be a good exercise? I'm not sure I would ever show it to anyone, but who knows. It might crystallize my thinking in a way that makes it easier to communicate. But, there's no doubt that it would take quite a bit of time.

Quite a bit of time indeed. It was over ten years ago that I first wrote those words about "writing something," and I continued to think about it during the first half of 2009, mentioning it several times in my journal. I finally scheduled a personal retreat in June 2009 at Conception Abbey in Conception, Missouri, about two hours north of my home in the Kansas City suburbs. On that retreat, I began writing what you are now reading, and in doing so, I created a file on my computer entitled *2009 Writing Project* – which is still the name of the file I am adding to as I type these words.

My intention before I actually began writing was that I would not only begin, but also *finish*, in 2009. Obviously, that didn't happen; it's taken me a lot longer than I initially thought it would, a function of both my sporadic working on it (in some cases, a gap measured in *years*), and the writing itself just being considerably more time consuming that I ever dreamed it would be. But, my spiritual journey didn't resolve in 2009. The ten years since, while not nearly as fast-paced as the five years before them, still contain significant things that have affected my spiritual journey, things that I must write about for the story to be complete up to this point.

Over the years my intended audience for this writing expanded beyond just "those who knew me in my former life." When I began writing, I was nervous about coming out as no longer a conservative evangelical Christian. I envisioned my audience being largely from that camp, and I feared their rejection. Ten years later, I'm much more willing to take what comes as far as reactions to what I've written. So, while I'll admit that I've written some parts with a bit of fear and trembling, the good thing about it taking so long is I've just gotten more comfortable with my story, who I am, and where I've ended up.

But, as time passed and I met more people who were asking similar questions and going through a similar faith transition as I was, I began to think about this writing as something for *them*, to encourage them in their journey and help them not feel so alone. Some of you reading this may have experienced, or be currently experiencing, significant evolution in your faith, but like me, you haven't known exactly what to do with it or how to talk about it. I hope you find some solace as you read this book.

So, my audience ends up three-fold:

1. Fellow sojourners in faith transition, for encouragement.
2. Members of my former tribe, conservative evangelical Christians, for explanation of what's happened to me with a view towards expanding horizons regarding different expressions of faith.
3. Myself, for me to document and personally better understand my journey.

A few additional things I want to mention up front...

When I first began writing in 2009, I still referred to God as a "he." I certainly didn't think God was gendered by that point, but I was in the life-long habit of referring to God as masculine, driven by the church culture I was in and masculine biblical references (especially God the *Father* and Jesus the *Son*), and was not explicitly trying to change that. As time went on, I eventually eliminated gendered pronouns of God from my verbal and written vocabulary, but for continuity's sake, I have retained referring to God as "he" throughout this entire book. Just know that if referring to God as masculine offends you in any way, that I don't really think that way or mean it now. In fact, in most ways now, if I think of gender in association with the divine, I am more inclined to think in feminine images rather than masculine ones (and there is certainly Scripture to support feminine images of God).

I also want to acknowledge the privilege associated with this writing. I have literally spent hundreds of hours – perhaps *thousands* – thinking and writing about my spiritual journey. You will see soon enough that it was at times a very painful path for me. However, I recognize that pain is relative, and mine is relative to an overall easy and fortunate life. I have never had to worry about food, shelter or safety. I also have always had supportive, loving people around me. So, I recognize that the context for my spiritual journey is one of privilege, high up on Maslow's Hierarchy of Needs. That said, it doesn't make the trauma of some of what I experienced less real. And, I'm guessing that most of you reading this are living at a similar level of privilege. Let's just acknowledge that in not only the full course of human history, but even among the billions living today, that we are fortunate that we can even pay attention to and spend time thinking and talking about such things as our thoughts and feelings about faith and spirituality.

A note about structure: I have written in mostly chronological order. I am largely a linear thinker, and so this is the order that made most sense to me. There are a few exceptions, but the first chapter starts shortly after my birth in 1963, and chapter ten ends with where I am now in late 2019. There are undoubtedly other ways – perhaps better ways – to write a story like mine, but this is how I've done it.

If you are a conservative evangelical Christian, I want to warn you that some – maybe a lot – of what you will read might make you uncomfortable. The story of how my faith has evolved is one that includes an unblinking look at – and at times a withering critique of – conservative evangelical Christianity. If you are happy in your faith, or sensitive to critiques of it, this might be a book you should consider skipping.

Finally, regardless of where you stand in relation to faith and spirituality, I hope you come away from reading this with a broader appreciation for the variety of spiritual paths that people can take. Ultimately, all of us who have some spiritual awareness and yearning just want to feel connection and union with other people and with this Mystery we sometimes call God. I hope any doctrinal concerns you might have are superseded by a provocation to immerse yourself more fully in community and Mystery.

# 1: 1963 – 1995

In many ways, my childhood was pretty idyllic. I grew up on a farm near Caldwell, Kansas, a half mile north of the Kansas-Oklahoma border southwest of Wichita, with my mom, dad, and sisters Debbie (seven years my senior) and Kristi (five years my junior). Our farm house was smack dab in the middle of a full section of land, which is one square mile, so our "driveway" was a half of a mile long. Our farmstead had lots of farm buildings, trees, open areas of grass, and old abandoned farm equipment. All of these fueled my imagination into a full range of play activities, none better than the old rusted abandoned combine that could be any number of things, from spaceships to evil fortresses.

My dad was a wheat farmer, in partnership with his brother, my uncle Glen. By the age of 12, I spent my summers working for them full-time on the farm, harvesting the wheat in June, and in July and August spending 12 hours a day, 6 days a week, riding round and round in fields in a tractor pulling a disc, plow, or, God forbid, the old Krause chisel that was always breaking down and was the bane of my existence. My dad and my uncle Glen could have bad tempers in the midst of trying to make a living farming, but most of the time were great to work for. From them I learned to work hard, do things right, laugh and cuss. I've put all of those to good use over the years.

My mom and dad provided a very stable and accepting household for my sisters and me. My older sister Debbie was born with spina bifida, had a urostomy, and was essentially paralyzed from the waist down. She struggled off and on with health problems her entire life. She could be emotionally volatile, but was also a lot of fun. My sister Kristi and I entertained her with silly songs and skits, and usually coaxed her to be part of them. She was an easy laugh. As an adult she was able to work at a sheltered workshop in nearby Wellington, and even finally moved into a group home there, giving my mom somewhat of a break after three decades of constant daily caregiving. Debbie died at the age of 42 of a brain aneurysm on my 35th birthday. Yes, I know that sounds sad, and it certainly is. But, she wasn't supposed to make it past infancy; in fact, the attending doctor advised my parents to not take her home from the hospital so that they wouldn't get too attached to her.

Caldwell was classic small-town rural America. It had only about 1,500 people living in the town and surrounding area. My graduating class of 1981 had 30 people. The class after mine, 1982, the class of my girlfriend Michelle and my best friend and cousin Russ, was a *big* class, as it had 32 graduates. There wasn't a lot to do in Caldwell, outside of school activities. I was a sporadic participant in school sports, but began learning to play the guitar in eighth grade, and formed a rock band called *Force* with Russ, who learned guitar at the same time I did. We were ax-slinging adolescents trading off guitar solos and lead vocals for an audience that could only be described as small and undiscerning. But man, we had fun.

Despite the small size, Caldwell had a lot of churches, over ten, I think. My family were members of the Caldwell United Methodist church. I didn't think about or understand what made our church different than any other church in town. We definitely had the largest and coolest building, with beautiful old stained-glass windows and an awesome pipe organ. I certainly knew there was something different and somewhat mysterious about the Catholics, but I really didn't know what it was. But as far as substantive differences between the churches, I couldn't have told you, and I don't suspect many others – children or adults – could have either. Going to church was just something you did, and you went to a certain church because that's where your parents went, and your grandparents before them, and so on.

I didn't know it then, but now I know that my Methodist church was a fairly typical '60s – '70s mainline small-town church. The church was more social than overtly spiritual, political, or transformational. Having an ongoing personal relationship with God was not something that was talked much about, nor was how our faith was supposed to shape our individual lives or our lives together. The general impression I was left with was that God resided primarily in the church building itself, and that our duty to God was to visit him there once a week. Not that I didn't sense him and pray to him at times other than at church. But, he was not integral in my ongoing day-to-day life, and did not have a clear, conscious influence on the choices I made.

I do remember two instances of Sunday School teachers, in late grade school or junior high, initiating discussion about how faith and God apply in a world where an awful lot of bad things happen, and expressing some doubts in their faith. I didn't know how, or wasn't inclined, to engage in that type of conversation then. And soon, I would be plunged into a religious environment where those kinds of doubts would be submerged under platitudes of positivity, and looked at as a pure lack of faith and spiritual maturity. Now I look back at those as signs of vulnerability, humanity, and resilience, but I'm already getting ahead of myself.

*The Awakening*

As I got into my teens, my awareness of God grew, as did my awareness of girls and various other pleasures of life. I distinctly remember praying every night a somewhat rote prayer that included a blessing for my mom and dad and a request to not get sick and throw up (to this day, I really detest vomiting, and will go to somewhat ridiculous extremes to try to avoid it). None of my friends and classmates talked much about God, although my girlfriend Michelle clearly had a more intimate relationship with God than I did. God remained largely on the margins of my life until my senior year of high school.

As I think was typical of most small-town churches at the time, women did practically everything in my church except preach (all the pastors of my home church were male until the '90s). Our youth group leaders were women, and for many of those years, included my mom. The women tried, God bless 'em, but youth group was largely a microcosm of the church as a whole: primarily social, with little content that made any of us think seriously about God and how he fit into our lives (although I'm open to the idea now that I and others like me just weren't listening or paying attention all that well). But a new family moved to town the summer before my senior year, and they had a college age son named Bob who volunteered to help with the youth. He became my first official personal encounter with the conservative evangelical version of Christianity.

I will never forget the first time I met Bob and heard him speak. We were having a youth group party at the Caldwell bowling alley at the beginning of my senior year. After all the games had been bowled, Bob was introduced. He didn't say much that day, mostly just introductory comments, but I distinctly remember these words: *I'm not like most guys you know my age, I'm a born-again Christian.* I don't think I had heard the words "born again Christian" come out of someone's mouth before, and I sure didn't know what they meant. But, they stayed with me.

Throughout my senior year, I got to know Bob better, and it was clear that he *was* different, and different in ways that were increasingly attractive to me. The phrase I used with a friend was that Bob seemed to have it "all together." With leaving home for college looming, I felt more and more like I was floundering and directionless, while Bob seemed to have definite passion, purpose, and direction to his life. As the year progressed, it was becoming clearer to me that God and I were not completely on the same wave length. He was still on the periphery of my life, but I was now aware of that, and even more, aware that he wanted a bigger role. A moment of truth – a literal "come to Jesus" event – was inevitable.

It came in May at the end of the school year, when a bunch of us senior guys went to a local lake to camp and to celebrate graduating by getting totally trashed (a keg of beer for about 12 of us – this was not just to have a beer or two with our campfire dinner). I did what I came to do, ending up not only completely wasted but sick as well (yes, the despised throwing up). As I went from tree to tree by the lake regurgitating beer and hot dogs, my physical sickness was mirrored by an unmistakable soul sickness. I was sick of living life at odds with God, and living by and large for the next time I could get drunk with my friends. I cried, told God I was sorry, and invited him "into my heart," an idea that I had become aware of through Bob's influence in the youth group. I was inviting God to no longer stay at the margins of my life, but to be at the center – the heart – of it.

Even though I was certainly a bit inebriated, I was sincere that day by the lake, and God took me at my word. Little by little, and sometimes by leaps at a time, he became more and more integral to my life throughout that summer after my senior year. Some of this was initiated by me, but much of it just kind of happened to me. I found that I was just so much more aware of God, and I couldn't ignore him any longer. I began to pray more often and more spontaneously, and I began reading the Bible for the first time in my life. I sensed God alive and working and speaking to me, and it was exciting. Life felt fresh, new, and purposeful.

As leaving for my freshman year of college drew near, I finally got up the nerve to tell my youth leader Bob about what was happening to me. It happened after a youth group event at a member's cabin on the Chikaskia River in Drury, a tiny little river community near Caldwell. I hesitantly approached Bob as he was walking to his car to leave and told him what was going on in my life. He was very accepting of me, encouraged me to keep reading the Bible and seek out committed Christian groups in college, and really became my first true "Christian" friend. And although I didn't realize or understand it at the time, that conversation also officially inducted me into the stream of the Christian faith known as conservative evangelicalism.

*Belonging, Believing, Behaving*

In August of 1981, I packed up my red '79 Firebird and traveled an hour northeast to Wichita, Kansas, where I began my freshman year at Wichita State University. One of the first things I noticed and experienced right away was its diversity, especially racial. Caldwell was very homogeneous, being almost exclusively white. Living on my dorm floor my freshman year were farm kids, suburban kids, and city kids; multiple black football players, including the starting fullback who became a friend; band nerds, including an African American one; a suitemate from South America; the kicker on the football team from Mexico; several black track athletes, including my eventual roommate, good friend and usher at my wedding (and yes, a black usher at a wedding in Caldwell was indeed a very rare occurrence); and future NBA

All-Star Xavier McDaniel. The full mixing of athletes and non-athletes in the dorms greatly facilitated this kind of diversity, which I quickly not only got comfortable with, but really enjoyed. And, it was a diversity that I would struggle to duplicate in any setting the rest of my life. Looking back, I think I assumed that because we all appeared to get along so well that we had arrived at some sort of colorblind society. I never thought to ask my many black friends and acquaintances if they experienced any discrimination because of the color of their skin. Now I know they undoubtedly did, they just hid it well, or just as likely, I wasn't paying close enough attention.

Generally speaking, my college and early adult years were all about me becoming more deeply rooted in conservative evangelical Christianity. It was also certainly true that during these years I was becoming closer to God and more aware of his presence and activity in my life. But just as importantly, I was learning to belong, believe, and behave within the evangelical wing of the Christian faith.

First and foremost, I found a new group of people to hang out with and belong to. These were people who were very accepting of me and expressed great joy that I was part of their group. I didn't take me long at Wichita State to find a Christian community. Early on I met a guy named Lewis who lived in my dorm and led a weekly Bible study, of which I became a regular attendee. Fellowship of Christian Athletes also met in my dorm's common area, and many non-athletes, including me, regularly attended. I got exposed to contemporary Christian music, and became an avid listener. I discovered Christian radio and popular conservative Christian teachers like John MacArthur, Chuck Swindoll, and Charles Stanley.

After I married my high school sweetheart Michelle mid-way through my junior year of college, we joined an Evangelical Free church in Wichita, the first truly conservative evangelical church we ever attended. We got involved in Sunday School and a Navigators 2:7 class. We moved to Dallas and quickly found an evangelical church, becoming highly involved in Sunday School, study-intensive discipleship groups, and home-based small groups. We made friends in these churches that loved us, accepted us, supported us, encouraged us, and with whom we just had lots of fun. Some of these people are the kind of friends that you make at crucial points in your life, and will remain friends for a lifetime. Some of you are reading this now.

Finding this new group I could belong to – people that shared my newfound faith and the beliefs and values that came with it – was very important to my developing relationship with God. The people with whom I attended church, Bible studies, small groups, and Sunday School – and the larger conservative evangelical community as well – became my community and family. I made significant lifelong friends during this formative time, and I will be forever grateful for this. But there was a dark side as well, unbeknownst to me at the time, and it was this: it was an exclusive club. There were very specific beliefs and behaviors that gained you entrance or got you expelled. That may well be the case with any group one could ever be part of, but it was certainly true with the evangelical community.

The naïve, fresh interactivity of my first months of faith – where God seemed vital and alive and real moment by moment – slowly but surely gave way to a codified system of belief. Now don't get me wrong: it's not that having an ongoing interactive relationship with God was unimportant to evangelical faith; in fact, quite the contrary. But, as I got into the Bible studies and classes, the personal relationship side seemed to be increasingly dwarfed by the very specific right and wrong ways to believe and think about God and how he works and makes himself known to people. In other words, I learned doctrine, and specifically, the conservative evangelical variety, and the utter importance of it.

Of course, all of this doctrine was based on the Bible. One of the hallmarks of evangelical faith is to have at least one Bible verse backing up every doctrine. I didn't comprehend at the time that there was a whole lot of picking and choosing of what verses really matter and which ones don't. What made evangelical doctrine stick with me was that people who loved me and that I really trusted told me it was absolutely true, and that Scripture clearly stated the right way to believe and think about God, life, humanity, the world, and eternity.

And, doctrinally speaking, eternity was *the* thing. Granted, not the *only* thing; evangelicals did plenty of good works to help people in the here and now (and continue to do so; in fact, perhaps now more than ever, as eternity seems to have lost at least some of its evangelical doctrinal preeminence vs. 30-35 years ago). But ultimately, it was what happens to you after you die that was of utmost importance. It's interesting in thinking back to my initial reading of the New Testament that summer between my senior year in high school and my freshman year in college, prior to deep immersion in the evangelical culture; I didn't come away thinking that eternity was all that matters. But in the evangelical literature I read (including Chick tracts, with its horrifying cartoon drawings of hell) and the people I met in the Bible studies and the churches, it became pretty clear that what happens in eternity was of supreme importance. Specifically, the most central belief – the doctrine above all doctrines – was this: accept Jesus as your personal Lord and Savior and be saved and go to heaven when you die, and if you don't, you are lost and will go to hell where you will burn for all eternity.

So, being a Christian meant that you literally believed this. And, if you cared at all about people you knew that were not Christians like you, you needed to make it a priority to tell them about Jesus and do whatever you can to save them. I took this very seriously for the first few years, trying to work Jesus into every conversation with friends and acquaintances. In the process, I damaged some of my old friendships by trying to pressure and scare them into "accepting Christ." I even tried to tell complete strangers about Jesus. I did this because it was just what you were supposed to do. But I must admit, it was never natural or comfortable to me. It often resulted in the other person feeling violated and offended. Likewise, I usually came away from these encounters feeling like I had in some way violated the other person, that I had crossed some line of common decency in spiritually accosting them. But I was taught to ignore this feeling; the greater good – the other person's salvation from eternal damnation – demanded it.

Regardless, a few of my friends did profess faith in Christ directly or indirectly from my conversations with them. While that was very exciting initially, their newfound faith generally didn't last very long. Most of my old friends just ignored me and my pleas for their conversion. That set up the following problem: after you have tried to talk to all your friends and acquaintances about Jesus and they all rebuff you, what you are left with is a lot of rejection and guilt. *I obviously am not doing this right, or praying enough before my conversations, or relying on the Holy Spirit enough!* This really haunted me early on in my faith.

I remember one day in college coming to the alarming realization that I had never really truly talked to one of my best friends about Jesus. He obviously knew about my new faith; I completely wore it on my sleeve and so it was hard to miss. But I had never engaged him in an intentional conversation about it. This put me in quite a dilemma: according to the theology I had been taught and embraced at the time, I needed to go talk to him about Jesus as soon as possible! I didn't want to do it, because I knew that it would add tension to our already strained relationship. But, if I was really a Christian, what choice did I have? Did I want it on my conscience that he spends eternity in flames because I was too scared to talk to him?

So, after much internal agonizing, I went over to his dorm, took the elevator up to his floor, walked hesitantly down the hall to his room, knocked on the door, and nervously waited for him to answer. He never did. I was simultaneously thrilled and depressed! I never did have that conversation with him. But looking back, I can say that day was a turning point in my views on and efforts in evangelism. Specifically, only a few years into my conservative faith, it was the beginning of the end of my evangelistic intensity.

Related to issues of eternity was the mania of the end times in the '70s and early '80s. I read Hal Lindsay's *The Late Great Planet Earth* and saw the film *A Thief in The Night* – musts for evangelicals at that time. Conservative Christianity was all abuzz over prophecy, the book of Revelation, and the impending rapture, tribulation, and end of the world as we know it. Being a true Christian meant you believed wholeheartedly in these things, and that Jesus could and would come back at any time.

But the conservative dogma requirements didn't end there. Through Bible studies, church classes, Christian radio, etc., I learned the "right" ways to think about God, Jesus's purpose and death, the Holy Spirit, God's sovereignty vs. free will, the Bible, and a host of other doctrines. I was taught to memorize Scripture verses that backed up many of these doctrines, and defend them to skeptics. But it didn't stop with belief. Behaviors were also of primary concern.

There were definite behaviors that were considered good and bad. I quickly learned that drinking alcohol, drugs, any form of premarital sexual contact (not just intercourse, but anything beyond basic kissing), smoking, and any cuss words whatsoever were strictly forbidden. Secular music was of the devil and should be avoided, as should most movies and TV shows. Church attendance, a daily quiet time, working Jesus into your everyday speech and every conversation, targeting friends and acquaintances for evangelism, etc. – these were the good behaviors. While much of this has eased up within evangelical Christianity over the years, there are still considerable expectations in many circles regarding acceptable and unacceptable behavior, including matters that are strictly or primarily personal and private and have little-to-no impact on anyone else.

Although I became largely indoctrinated into this believe-and-behave form of conservative Christianity, I didn't go so far as to not have my share of fun. I generally didn't violate the prescribed behavior guidelines (at least not severely), but there were certain people – and mostly other Christians – that I just plain had fun with. We didn't feel the need to throw God into every sentence or conversation. We just had good clean fun, laughed a lot, and enjoyed life – the life that God had given us.

But, that set up a contrast between my serious friends and my fun friends, and ultimately between two ways of living and being a Christian. One way was all about being very careful with what you believed and how you behaved. Entertaining any doubt or dabbling in any belief or philosophy outside of conservative Christian theology could lead you down the slippery slope of liberalism, heresy, and unbelief. Any slip in behavior (known as "backsliding") would ruin your testimony for Christ, and lead you down the slippery slope of hedonism, addiction, and godlessness.

The other way of living and being a Christian was much more carefree and fun-loving, living more in the moment and from the heart – much more akin to those first few months of my faith. It was obviously a more enjoyable and less stressful way to live. But, if I perceived I was doing it too much, I would feel guilty for spending my life and time on "lesser things" that distracted me from doing what I was really supposed to be doing, which was paying close attention to my beliefs and behavior and telling as many people as possible about Jesus lest they burn in hell for eternity. This was just a small tension early on in my faith, but it was a harbinger of things to come, planting the seeds that would eventually grow to be a key issue in my faith journey years later.

*Ministry*

I knew early on in my faith that I was not just expected to receive blessings from God and from others. I was expected to give back. In the beginning, this was primarily about evangelism, telling others about Jesus. It took me awhile to figure out that I wasn't very good at this. But, eventually I saw that there were other things I could do reasonably well to give back to God, to serve him and the church – otherwise known as *ministry*.

The version of evangelicalism I was part of emphasized the priesthood of all believers. We were all ministers, not just those who were paid to deliver sermons, counsel parishioners, and visit members when they were in the hospital. But, I struggled to know how I fit, how specifically I could minister to others. I had been writing and performing songs for years, so it was natural for me to now write and perform songs from a faith perspective. But quite frankly, my early attempts at this didn't elicit the kind of response from others that I had hoped for, and so my musical efforts faded away for a number of years.

In my early 20s, as I transitioned from primarily a college Christian community to an "official" institutional church, I felt very intimidated by the other Christians I met there. I was a newly married adult, 21 years old, still in college and with no career. The "young" Christians I met at the church were very nice, but plain and simple, they were older and at different life stages. I felt like I had little in common with them, and felt like a little kid around them. Being with people that are five, ten, fifteen years older than you is not a big deal when you're 50, but I found it pretty daunting at 21.

I remember the first week attending a "young marrieds" Sunday School class in our church in Wichita. We got into small groups and had to briefly tell something about ourselves. I shared that I was a student at Wichita State. The guy next to me, who was obviously much older than me, shared that he was a *professor* at Wichita State. He found that rather humorous and ironic; I found it humiliating and felt like the butt of a cruel joke.

All of this greatly affected my confidence for a few years in my early 20s. We moved to Dallas in 1986 when I was 23 to take my first "real" job at a marketing research firm. I was still younger and less advanced career-wise than most of the other "young" folks at our church, but there was less distance between us than was the case in Wichita. However, the large presence of students from Dallas Theological Seminary (DTS) intimidated me and offset any other gain in confidence, at least for a couple of years. They seemed to know a lot more than I did, and it didn't help that I had some doctrinal struggles and confusion here and there over issues like charismatic gifts (*did I really have the full gift of the Holy Spirit if I didn't speak in tongues like some Christians I knew, who seemed happier and more "spiritual" than I did?*) and human free will vs. God's sovereignty. But I gradually grew more confident and felt less inferior, and became more vocal in Sunday School and in our small group.

The small group we attended was led by a very smart and gracious DTS student. He and his wife became great friends of ours, and he took me under his wing, encouraging me to lead Bible discussions at some of the meetings. His encouragement and support led me to eventually start a small group in our suburb of Irving. It was a very successful group that I started from the ground up, calling everyone in the church directory with an Irving area address. We filled the group in no time, and it boosted my confidence substantially.

One important thing that happened during my time in Dallas was being introduced to contemporary praise and worship music. The music at the church services that I had grown up with, as well as the ones at our Evangelical Free church in Wichita, were predominantly hymns. The choir would break out something a bit more contemporary once in a while, but the congregation didn't get to participate in those. Congregational participatory music-based worship was exclusively hymns, most of which were at least 100 years old.

I will never forget my first visit to our Dallas church, Fellowship Bible Church, a nondenominational contemporary evangelical church. There was no choir loft, no large pulpit, no altar, no pews. Rather, there were padded chairs in a semicircle surrounding a platform that included a piano and drum set. A bassist, guitarist, and a couple of vocalists joined the pianist and drummer. The sound they produced was like nothing I had heard previously in a church, and it lifted me into the heavenly realms like nothing I had experienced before.

This was momentous for two reasons. One, it introduced me to a more emotional side of faith and relationship with God. The conservative evangelical Christianity that I had been part of up to this point was decidedly intellectual, logical, rational and word-based. Reading, dissecting, memorizing, and theologizing the Bible was what the faith was primarily about. Finding this new form of music that helped me lift my heart to God and have spiritual union with him beyond sheer doctrine and theology was refreshing and invigorating to my soul. This made my faith much better rounded, and provided me with a significant outlet to communion with God for years to come. It also gave me a vision for future ministry. I had played guitar and sung for years, back to my teenage years fronting *Force*, but these abilities sat relatively dormant during the first half of my 20s. These would come back to life in a big way a few years later.

By early 1989, Michelle and I were both getting restless in Dallas. My career was not going as well as I wanted, so I began making plans to go to graduate school. Michelle and I had been trying to get pregnant for well over a year, with no success. So, we put our house on the market, I took the GMAT and began applying to graduate schools outside of Dallas, and guess what? We got pregnant. We were thrilled, and decided to proceed with our graduate school plan. So, in August 1989, with Michelle seven months pregnant, we rented a Ryder truck and drove across the hot, humid south to Athens, Georgia so I could get a Master's degree in Marketing Research at the University of Georgia. Our first child, our daughter Erin, was born that November (her grandpap liked to called her a Georgia peach). While I was completing my degree, I led a Bible Study among my fellow graduate students, something I could not have done without the confidence gained leading small groups at our church in Dallas.

After completing my degree, Michelle, Erin (now seven months old), and I moved to Kansas City where I started working as a Marketing Research Analyst at Hallmark Cards in the summer of 1990. We felt immediately at home in Kansas City. We quickly found a church, Oakbrook Church, and settled in, having two more children, our son Jordan in March '92 and our daughter Haley in May '94.

Oakbrook Church was a relatively small conservative nondenominational church that did contemporary worship similar to our church in Dallas. It didn't take me too long to get involved in the music ministry, eventually leading it, and sharing weekly worship leader duties with one other person, and I continued to regularly experience God's presence and pleasure through contemporary praise and worship music.

But Oakbrook included some people who were serious doctrine watchdogs. The tension between the more emotional praise and worship time of the service and Bible-based teaching and doctrine that happened during the sermon and in Sunday School was decidedly greater than in our church in Dallas. During my time in charge of the music, more than once someone in the congregation called me out about songs that were deemed as doctrinally incorrect, putting me in a position of having to defend my song choices. One of these men was speaking at a men's retreat that I was attending, and to my surprise and without my advanced notice or permission, he started telling the men about his efforts to ban a song (which he successfully did, by the way). He positioned it as him "contending for the faith that the Lord has delivered once for all to the saints" (Jude 3). I was blindsided by it, and it is my first memory of feeling publicly ostracized due to dogma, by someone who felt it was their role to play doctrine police and protect the people from the heretical influence of the lyrics to fluffy worship tunes.

Not that I was innocent in this area. In the early '90s we became friends with a couple at our church whose children were similar in age to ours, and who were also asking similar questions as us about the church at large and its calling and role in the world. But something unexpected happened with the husband along the way: he began to ask deeper, more fundamental questions about Christianity itself, including whether all the books and writers contained in the Scriptures were truly inspired by God. Being by now a staunch adherent and advocate of conservative Christianity, I didn't know what to do with all this. It baffled me. Once people were "in," they were supposed to stay "in" and get stronger in their faith, not regress into what I perceived as faithless questions and doubts.

Ultimately, I felt deceived by my friend. I thought he was something (a well-grounded, orthodox, conservative, evangelical Christian) that he was not, and I told him this. This hurt him deeply, and our relationship would never recover. I offered to meet with him regularly to talk through his questions, but honestly, my motive was to reform him, and he undoubtedly sensed that and we never met. So, while I regretted hurting him and the dissolution of our friendship, I was fully convinced I was right. I was merely "contending for the faith" with Jude and the retreat speaker. But in reality, by judging him in the same way I felt judged by the retreat speaker, I was fulfilling the Apostle Paul's words: "At whatever point you judge another, you are condemning yourself, because you who pass judgment do the same things" (Romans 2:1). This would become even more apparent years down the road, as I myself would begin asking questions that would go far beyond the ones my friend was asking.

Throughout the early-to-mid-'90s, I was generally in a restless place spiritually. I read books by Chuck Colson that made me think more about how we should be helping the poor and oppressed, which I didn't see a church largely obsessed with eternity doing much of, and I certainly wasn't doing much of either. I read books about the cell church and small group movement, and became convinced that the church should be oriented around small/cell groups and that *every* Christian should be part of one. Generally speaking, I increasingly thought the church at large was broken and desperately needed fixing.

Eventually, in 1995, I began reading books and listening to recordings by Rick Warren and Bill Hybels on the purpose-driven and seeker church movements. I had not engaged in much significant individual evangelism for years. I had essentially given up on it, but certainly felt guilty, about both not doing it and giving up on it. Warren and Hybels gave me a new vision for doing evangelism not so much individually, but corporately as a whole church.

Once I got the seeker church bug, there was no turning back. I needed to be part of this new expression of church. I felt that God was calling me to do this, and so I set out to find a local Kansas City church that was committed to being seeker-targeted. The first seeker church I visited was a fairly large and prominent seeker church not far from my house. But it was clearly a "done deal" there, with over 1,000 attending, a full staff, and mostly professional musicians doing the worship. I didn't want to just go and be a spectator. I wanted to be integral to the entire process and help shape what a church was all about, which would have been nearly impossible at that church. So, I continued the search, and it didn't take me long to find the one I was looking for.

# 2: 1996 – 2003

The same month I started my job in the Business Research department at Hallmark in Kansas City, a fresh-faced kid from Virginia named Chris joined the company in the same department. As the years went on, we gradually became friends, and the topic of God and church eventually came up. He told me his story, about moving from Virginia and meeting someone at the Hallmark fitness center that he vaguely knew from college who invited him to this new church that met in a school. Chris and his wife Lori would not have called themselves committed Christians prior to visiting this church, but they loved it and the people they met there. Soon they committed their lives to Christ, got baptized and became heavily involved. Chris credited this church for at least jumpstarting his and Lori's dormant faith.

As I searched for a seeker church in the spring of 1996, Chris's church – RidgePoint Christian Church, an independent nondenominational Christian church (rather than a denominational Disciples of Christ church, also generally called a Christian Church) – was definitely on the radar screen. I distinctly remember my first visit to RidgePoint. It was six years old and still meeting in a middle school, but with building plans on the near horizon. I remember what the pastor Brad talked about that day. I remember who else had roles in the service, and I remember Chris's guitar playing. And above all, I remember the feeling I had during and after it: that I was supposed to be part of it.

Over the next two months, I prayed and discussed all of this at length with Michelle, and I took her, Erin, Jordan, and Haley to visit. We ultimately both felt that God was calling us to RidgePoint. So, we left our old church and began attending RidgePoint that summer, and we jumped in with both feet. Before long we joined a small group. I became involved with the music and was soon put in charge of it. I also joined a team that decided the content of the Sunday morning seeker services, known as the Programming team.

I found my ministry groove at RidgePoint in a short amount of time. Within a few months of being there, I took a class to discover my spiritual gifts and my area of passion, something I had never done before. The results all made intuitive sense: I found that I was gifted in leadership and administration, and that my passion was the church. But, the interesting part was what the person who was leading the class told me about my passion. She said that only a few people she knew of had a passion for the church – and they were all on-staff pastors at RidgePoint. It was the first time I remember wondering if eventually I would be in full-time professional paid ministry. Those thoughts would come to me more and more over the coming few years.

*The Calling*

By the spring of 1999, I was in a bad place professionally. I was now working for a marketing research firm, where I had risen very quickly within the company the previous three years. After a couple of years of success running the Kansas City branch office, at the age of 35, I was promoted to Vice President in charge of half the company's six branch offices. But, the company was not doing very well, and my three branch offices were no exception. The Kansas City and Dallas branches were barely holding their own, but the San Francisco branch was in a total free-fall, with clients and employees abandoning ship weekly. I found myself traveling to the Bay area at least every other week trying to salvage what I could. Because of this frequent travel, I had to drop most of my volunteer activity at RidgePoint, which was very depressing to me. I was very disillusioned with my career, I was away from my family a lot, and I didn't have any free time to devote to volunteer ministry. I hated it. This was the state I found myself in when the first call came from pastor Brad about Mission Possible.

18

Mission Possible was a campaign to raise money to add two-to-three RidgePoint staff members. Brad called asking me to consider a Director of Ministries position, which was largely administrative. This position didn't really excite me very much. However, another position to be added did: Director of Creative Arts and Programming. This person would be responsible for everything that happened on stage in all worship services except the sermon, and I expressed my interest in it. Another person Brad was talking to about that position fairly quickly turned him down, and so he was very amenable to talking with me about the position. After some negotiation, we settled on terms and I started on-staff at RidgePoint on August 1, 1999.

In the past, I always liked to say I was called by God to full-time paid ministry, and specifically to RidgePoint and the particular position of Director of Creative Arts and Programming, and I don't want to necessarily rule this out altogether. But, I also know that my state of mind at the time was one of desperately wanting to escape my current situation. So, I was ripe for the picking. I guess I'm now content to say that the combination of my need to do something different at the time, my availability, my specific gifts and skills, and RidgePoint's needs were a good match, and perhaps God had some involvement in all that (although I'm certainly less clear about that now than I was then).

The people of RidgePoint were generally thrilled with my decision to go on-staff (there might have been a few dissenters and skeptics, but if so, they kindly kept their doubts and opposition to themselves). The Creative Arts/Programming area had needed some focused leadership for some time, and so I was welcomed with open arms. And as such, there was a significant honeymoon period for me in that position. During my first couple of years on the job, the Creative Arts team became a more supportive, intimate community. Through Creative Arts' and my leadership, RidgePoint became much more of a "worshipping church" (contemporary evangelical-speak for people becoming more visibly engaged and animated during praise and worship singing, along with the testimony that they were having more real and palpable experiences with God through it). The church experienced numeric growth during this time, and the people coming in were on board and generally happy to be part of it all. It was evident that God was in our midst and at work. It was an exciting, fulfilling time for the church and for me personally.

One thing I did fairly early on was tighten up some of the language we used to explain communion, which we took every Sunday and was part of my area of responsibility. In my early years at RidgePoint, I struggled with some of the church's doctrines, or lack thereof. The church I had just come from had a number of devoted doctrinaires, and under their influence and a somewhat steady diet of conservative Christian radio and books, I had become more and more theologically rigid on certain issues over the years. RidgePoint was not nearly as buttoned-up theologically as I would have liked. This was evident in some of my very early conversations with some of the pastors and leaders, before we had fully committed to joining RidgePoint. One big issue for me then was the role of water baptism: was baptism necessary for someone to be "saved?" They would not give me a clear unambiguous answer. In addition, sometimes various people at RidgePoint would say things that made it sound like salvation was at least partially through works, which was anathema at the churches I had previously attended. This perceived theological sloppiness didn't sit well with me, and over time, I was determined to change it as I had opportunity.

Various people gave the communion explanations at RidgePoint, and these explanations were very inconsistent, which I viewed as problematic. I considered our weekly communion explanation as an opportunity to "go to the cross" every week. It was perhaps our only chance in a given service to explain the "gospel," which to me at that time was completely about Jesus's death. Specifically, what that meant to me was a clear, concise explanation of penal substitutionary atonement (i.e., Jesus died in my place, paying the penalty that my sins deserved, fully absorbing God's punishment for my sins, making a way for me to be with God now and for eternity). In my view, this was the exclusive Biblical way to understand Jesus's "work" on the cross. I established language standards to try to make sure that substitutionary atonement was presented each and every week within the communion explanation. (The big irony of all this now is that a mere few years later, I would begin to deeply question the legitimacy of the penal substitutionary theory of the atonement, but again I'm getting ahead of myself.)

*The Letdown*

Similar to my previous job with the marketing research firm, after a couple of years of success as RidgePoint's Director of Creative Arts and Programming, signs of problems began to appear. In the fall of 2001, right on the heels of 9/11, we initiated another capital campaign, this one called Bridge to the Future. The goal: raise money to buy land. Our current facility was viewed as a decent "starter home," but not the kind of place where you'd want to settle down. And, if growth continued at the rate of the past couple of years, we were going to be out of room within the next five years. So, we embarked on a campaign to raise the money to buy land, and unlike the last campaign Mission Possible that was fully conceived, managed and executed by RidgePoint leadership, we hired a capital campaign consultant to help us do it.

I had some reservations about Bridge to the Future from the get-go. But pastor Brad and some others believed in it so much that I didn't have the nerve to say so, and the analysis regarding our growth rate and space limitations had some legitimacy behind it. Just *some* legitimacy because, in actuality, the growth projections were based on the most optimistic of scenarios; we had seen the growth rate level off quite a bit over the six months or so prior to starting the campaign. But, as the new kid on the leadership and staff block, I thought it was my duty to support the efforts and vision of Brad and the other leaders, and so I kept my reservations to myself, and quite frankly, largely drank the we-need-land-and-a-new-building Kool-Aid.

By most standards, Bridge to the Future was a success. It culminated in May 2002 with a big banquet where Bill Hybels from Willow Creek Community Church in suburban Chicago (our role model church) came to speak. In spite of a tough post-9/11 economy, we raised all the money we set out to raise (which was a definite departure from Mission Possible, the campaign that brought me on-staff in 1999, where we raised only a fraction of what was hoped for). But capital campaigns tend to drive wedges in churches, and this one was no exception. Some people left. Some people did not leave immediately, but Bridge to the Future marked the onset of their grumbling, dissent, and ultimate departure.

By the time the banquet approached, a friend of mine and a key member of the worship team was becoming a somewhat vocal Bridge to the Future dissenter within RidgePoint. When it came time to staff the worship team for the banquet, he assumed he would be one of the vocalists. But I told him he couldn't be part of the worship team that night. My reasoning was that since he wasn't a supporter of the campaign, why should he be upfront leading worship at the event? In effect, being upfront helping lead worship said that you supported Bridge to the Future and the banquet, and since he clearly didn't – and he freely admitted that – he shouldn't be involved.

Excluding him from this event hurt him deeply. It essentially made him feel like an outsider, no longer a member of the team, an "other." His reasoning for wanting to be part of it: *I may not agree with everything that goes on, but this is my church, my community, my family, and I want to be an active participant in the family's activities and significant events.* I didn't fully grasp that reasoning then, or my power to exclude and hurt as the one in authority making decisions. A few years later, as my views began diverging from the church and its leadership, I would also feel like an "other" and would understand his point of view more fully.

The ending of Bridge to the Future in the late spring/early summer of 2002 served symbolically as the end of my honeymoon on-staff at RidgePoint. My eyes had been opened to the inner workings of running a church, and the flawed natures of those who ran them. My honeymoon with the people of RidgePoint, particularly the Creative Arts team, was over, as grumblings began among some over my song choices or my style of leadership.

Anger was becoming a mounting issue in my life. I noticed myself becoming increasingly angry for no apparent reason, or getting furious at the slightest frustrations. I remember doing a home project on the patio in back of my house. My youngest daughter Haley was doing something on the screened porch right next to the patio. I was having difficulty with this project, and all of a sudden, I got extremely angry and hit a patio table as hard as I could and screamed out in frustration. This surprised and scared Haley, who went running inside. The episode hit me like a two-by-four to the head. What could have possibly caused me to explode like that? I decided I had better find out.

I scheduled an appointment with a Christian counselor, the first one I'd ever visited. I only saw this counselor once, and in that one session he helped identify some root causes and gave me some ideas to help – and he did this all without once referring to Scripture. This is significant because a decade earlier I was convinced that anything related to counseling and psychology was, at best, completely unnecessary for Christians, and at worst, totally "of the devil." Christians had the Bible, the Holy Spirit, and "the sufficiency of Christ" (which was the title of a book by John MacArthur that I read in the early '90s which cemented my opinion then on the evils of psychology). With all those resources at our disposal, what more could Christians possibly need? They certainly didn't need any secular, godless mumbo jumbo to give direction that only God could give through his Holy Word. So, seeing a counselor – and one that didn't copiously spout Scripture – was tacit admission that my worldview had gradually evolved and was continuing to.

There were others factors contributing to slow but sure changes in my worldview. I had largely latent but definitely growing intellectual questions. Sometime in the early part of the new millennium, I was flipping through channels one evening and came across a show on PBS on evolution. At that time, I held to a "progressively" literal view of Genesis 1, considering the "days" of creation eras of time – and thus an earth that is several billion years old rather than 4,000-6,000 – instead of literal 24-hour days, but affirming the literal account otherwise. As such, I certainly didn't believe in evolution, which I viewed as being in clear contradiction to Scripture. I don't remember the specifics of the program. All I remember is that I found many of the arguments for evolution compelling and it really shook me up. It bothered me for several days. How could someone who had been a Christian as long as I have be shaken by this? The stress of this event faded away, but the core issues of faith vs. science and literal vs. non-literal readings of the Bible did not. They were there, dormant but definitely planted in my mind, waiting for a later time to pop up and be more fully dealt with.

Another thing was happening progressively more often: certain practices that were supposed to make me feel closer to God – and that had worked for me in the past – increasingly did less and less for me. Worship music is the best example of this. Since first experiencing contemporary praise and worship music at the Dallas church in the mid-'80s, I could generally expect to experience the presence of God through this practice. I became a worship music aficionado, and prolifically wrote worship songs during my first few years on-staff at RidgePoint, culminating in me recording my songs in my basement in

2002-2003 and self-releasing a CD in spring 2004 (many of the songs don't hold up well over time, but a few of them do). As such, on some level I came to rely on praise and worship music as a cornerstone of my experience with God.

But as the years went by, it became rarer and rarer that I would have a palpable experience with God through worship music. I didn't want to acknowledge this at first, but more and more this created tension within me. Not only was worship music what I was primarily relying on to experience God's presence in my life, but I was a worship *leader*. As a worship leader, I felt that I couldn't lead people into God's presence to worship if I wasn't going there myself. This represented another blow to my worldview, to my thinking that the same spiritual practices should not only continue to work throughout your life, but should actually work better as you matured in your faith.

Factors chipping away at my worldview were by no means limited to intellectual issues and the waning effect of certain spiritual practices. Over the years, I had seen several people come to RidgePoint who were new converts to the faith, full of excitement and energy for the things of God, and then within six months or so, they were gone from not only RidgePoint, but from the faith in general. Even more concerning were the cases of those who had been part of Christianity longer term and still eventually decided to punt. I did not consciously acknowledge it until later, but every time I saw an example of someone abandoning their faith, it wreaked havoc on my deeply held belief – with Bible verses to back it up – that once someone became a Christian they would not only stay one, but become a better and better one over time. And if they didn't, it was clearly and totally their own fault. They made a conscious decision to abandon God, which I didn't think was truly possible if they had *really truly* been born again in the first place.

But my deepest disillusionments came from observing some of the ones who ostensibly stayed Christians. Evidently, staying a self-proclaimed Christian does not mean you automatically become more Christian (i.e., Christlike) over time, and unfortunately, this seems to be the case even – perhaps especially – among Christian leaders. Over the years, across multiple Christian environments, I saw truth stretched, and even blatant lying, to support a personal or "spiritual" agenda. I heard good people who weren't perceived as being fully on board with the program slandered in private. I witnessed racist comments and attitudes. I saw Christians chasing wealth and spending the vast majority of their money on nicer and bigger cars and houses... and yet they tended to be the ones most highly esteemed, held up as great examples, and given leadership positions by the church. I saw Christian leaders cheat on their spouses. I saw a church leader, upon finding out about his wife's infidelity, refuse to consider forgiveness and reconciliation and ignore all counsel and rapidly pursue divorce. (I am *not* saying there are not good reasons for divorce; I'm merely saying that in all relationships we should give forgiveness and reconciliation a fighting chance prior to severing ties, especially a marriage.)

This all began to raise some big questions about the effectiveness of the Christian faith. While I fully affirmed that "all have sinned and fall short of the glory of God" (Romans 3:23), is this really what Jesus had in mind when he said "follow me?" Is this what Paul had in mind when he said that "anyone who is in Christ is a new creation" (2 Corinthians 5:17)? Again, this did not fully register with me until later, but just under the surface my belief that Christians were simply far better people than non-Christians was gradually being whittled away. And this applied to the church as well. Shouldn't being a part of a community of believers, where we encourage one another and "spur one another on toward love and good deeds" (Hebrews 10:24), make us exemplary as both a group and as individuals – at the very least, better than those who are not part of it?

A final blow in this area happened among church leadership in the spring of 2004. We were beginning to struggle as a church. We were no longer growing numerically, much of what we were doing was starting to feel tired, and we lacked a real compelling, cohesive vision. In the midst of a time of diagnosing our problems, one leader sharply challenged another's leadership abilities and character, to which that leader reacted very defensively. There were power struggles and meetings with elders to try to sort it all out. Their relationship would never recover, and it cast a pall over the church staff and leadership for some time afterwards.

But of all the assaults on my worldview, of all the disappointments and disillusionments, the biggest one turned out to be... me. Simply put, if I were brutally honest, I was a mere shadow of what I thought and dreamed I would be when I signed up for this Christianity thing over 20 years earlier. I had decidedly less joy, peace, purpose and passion than I had in my first few years as a Christian. I had dreamed that I would set the world ablaze for Christ, and win countless souls for eternity, of which I fell laughably short. And all the disappointing qualities I saw in other Christians, I could also see in the mirror. Like everything else at the time, I was not fully conscious of it, and certainly not yet ready to acknowledge it. But it was there. Disappointment and disillusionment over what I had become – or more accurately, what I had *not* become.

So, as I approached mid-2004, I was ripe for some kind of tumultuous event. My conservative Christian worldview was increasingly being challenged by the observations and experiences of life. My anger issues and increasing disillusionment were simply the logical fallout of my disappointments and the gradual erosion of my worldview. Something would have to give soon.

# 3: 2004

Summer at RidgePoint was a time of relative leisure. Our "ministry season" mirrored the school year, so the months of June, July and August were very different from September through May. The staff worked hard during the ministry year, holding both Sunday morning and mid-week services, running women's and men's Bible studies, launching and coaching small groups, etc. During the summer months, many of these ministries effectively went on hiatus (with the obvious exception of our Sunday services), and we viewed these months as an opportunity to take some well-deserved time off.

Not that the staff just took a three-month vacation (although most of us did generally take some extended time off). But summer brought about a decided change of pace and a different set of activities, giving us a chance to do some things that we just didn't have time to do during the busy ministry season. This usually included what author Stephen Covey calls *Sharpening the Saw*: engaging in intentional and slower paced activities individually and as a staff to recharge our batteries. It allowed us to pay some attention to our own souls, not just church members', as well as give us some space to think, pray, plan and prepare for the upcoming ministry season.

For me, I sometimes used the summer to heavy-up on my reading. Generally, when I wasn't actively involved in ministry, I was mostly looking for diversions (I took up fishing as an adult during my first couple of years on-staff), and reading for me at that time was mostly just that. Consequently, when I read, I mostly read novels or historical biographies. When I did read something that was overtly spiritual or theological in nature, it almost always directly related in some fashion to one of my ministries, and so had a very practical purpose. Summer tended to prompt me to search for and read a book or two like this, in hopes that it might stimulate my thoughts and motivation as I prepared for the new ministry season in the fall.

In June of 2004, I was looking through a ministry magazine one day and came across their book awards for the previous year. One of the books profiled intrigued me. It was called *The Emerging Church*, written by a really funky looking pastor from Santa Cruz named Dan Kimball. What caught my attention was a key question Kimball was asking and attempting to shed some light on: why were there so few people under 35 in American churches and Christianity these days, and what could be done to attract them?

The issue of younger adults being missing from church was not totally new to me. It was something that kept popping up over the previous couple of years. I heard people talk about it some at Willow Creek conferences, and Willow had launched a special worship service called Axis that targeted what they liked to call "20-somethings." I was also becoming increasingly aware of the absence of this age group at RidgePoint. Sure, there were a few there, but at a much lower percentage than in the population at large. And, the ones who were there almost exclusively came from churched backgrounds. I had done a congregational survey that revealed that *all* of this age group considered themselves Christians prior to coming to RidgePoint, vs. only two-thirds of older attendees. So, while our goal of turning the irreligious into devoted Christ-followers had worked at least on some level with baby boomers, it was clearly not working among younger adults. This began to concern me.

So, I snapped up Kimball's book, devoured it, and I was an instant convert to his diagnosis of and solutions to the problem. I was primed for that kind of response given:

- The growing realization that RidgePoint's way of "doing church" was not working for those under 35.

- RidgePoint was no longer growing numerically, having reached a plateau a year or two earlier.

- The lack of a tight agreed-upon church vision.

- The failure of the church staff and elders to make any discernable progress in the midst of the recent staff infighting and turmoil.

- My overall disappointment with RidgePoint and the church at large as a result of these things.

*Postmodernism*

Kimball's primary diagnosis of why church and Christianity were losing ground among young adults: *Postmodernism*. Postmodernism was not a new term or idea to me; again, I had heard someone talk about it at a Willow Creek conference, and had actually bought a book on it a year or two earlier that I hadn't gotten very far on. But Kimball's writing on it seemed fresh and brand new to me, and I totally ate it up. In his book he referenced another book called *A New Kind of Christian* by another pastor/author Brian McLaren, who also wrote compellingly about the subject of Postmodernism. (I didn't realize it with my first reading in early fall 2004, but *A New Kind of Christian* and Brian McLaren would turn out to be a very pivotal as I progressed through my spiritual journey.)

So, what in the world is Postmodernism? Understanding Postmodernism is not necessarily an easy task. But I soon learned through Kimball and McLaren that it's easier to understand if you first understand *Modernism*, which makes sense given the very name *Post*modernism implies that it comes *after,* or *out of,* or *in response to,* Modernism. Modernism was ushered in by the Renaissance, propelled and more fully defined by the Enlightenment, and reached its full head of steam with the Industrial Revolution. So, it has been the milieu of the Western world for about 500 years. Postmodernism emerged in Europe after World War II, and really started to significantly influence America in the past 40 or so years.

Both Modernism and Postmodernism are essentially worldviews. As a

Westerner thoroughly steeped in Modernism, it can be tricky understanding Modernism because you first have to recognize your *own Modernity*, which is difficult when you are totally immersed in it. Put another way, a worldview is essentially the *lens* through which you see life, reality, and the world at large. It's virtually impossible to see a lens when you are looking through it. Understanding your lens requires first being aware that there even *is* a lens, and then you must make the effort to take the lens away from your eye and examine it to see how it affects your view. This is a fairly daunting task, seemingly an impossible one for many, but one that I came to believe is essential for understanding ourselves, others, and the world we live in.

Foundational to this understanding is *epistemology*, the philosophy of knowledge, which deals with *how we know things*. Although epistemology is not the *only* thing that distinguishes between Modernism and Postmodernism, I think it is generally the *best* thing, especially in considering how it relates to religion, faith, and spirituality.

Modernism maintains that a single, absolute truth exists that applies universally. Historically within the Western world, this truth is monotheistic and Judeo-Christian, although throughout the Modern period it was also increasingly scientific. We have access to this truth through our intellect, reasoning, logic, and linear and systematic thinking. Therefore, truth is generally rational and propositional. Modernism is highly optimistic and confident of our ability to know and access this ultimate propositional truth, and thus operates with a high degree of *certainty*. Since truth can be known with certainty and applies to all universally, moral, religious and cultural uniformity is ideal and encouraged. These gains in knowledge and certainty result in human advancement and progress, which is unanimously viewed as good and expected.

Postmodernism, simply stated, is a rejection of Modernism. Specifically, it rejects that there is one single universal truth that applies to all that is independent of time, place, culture, context, and language. It recognizes that we all have a lens through which we view the world – influenced by time, place, culture, context, and language. This lens affects what we see and do not see, and thus how we know and apprehend truth. Knowledge of truth is gained not only through our intellect, but also through our emotions, intuition, relationships, and experiences. This multivalent view of truth produces epistemological *humility* rather than certainty. We will not know everything, and what we do "know" we hold loosely, not with absolute certainty, because we recognize that we have a subjective, biased, culturally-conditioned view and apprehension of truth. And that's okay. It's also okay that you see the world and truth differently that I do. Diversity, mystery and complexity are acknowledged, expected, and valued.

Arising out of the aftermath of World War II Europe, Postmodern philosophers saw the dangers of Modern certainty and progress first hand. Hilter's Germany was certain in their way of thinking about the world and the people in it, and they acted on this certainty by invading nations and killing millions. This nation was one of the most advanced societies in all the world, and they used their "advances" and "progress" to create machines and systems intent on eradicating entire groups of people. And to top it off, this was a "Christian" nation. If this is what "progress" and "certainty" and a "single, absolute, universal truth" brings, then perhaps it's time to reconsider the whole Modern project. Thus, Postmodernism was born.

So, what does all this have to do with younger adults not being part of Christianity or the church? First, Kimball's contention was that since we are in a period of transition between Modernism and Postmodernism, there is a wide mix of both worldviews in our culture. We can't just say there is a Postmodern generation born between certain years. But, because those under 35 are the first generation to grow up under a predominantly Postmodern influence, this general rule applies: the younger you are, the more Postmodern you are likely to be.

Second, both Kimball and McLaren argued that the American church is predominantly, hopelessly Modern in its approach and orientation. Rational, systematic, information-based approaches are used for teaching, learning, evangelism, theology, and spiritual growth and formation. Spiritual development is measured largely by how much you know. Church buildings are designed primarily for information dissemination – and are increasingly utilitarian, devoid of inherent beauty or symbolism. Multifaceted, paradoxical, mysterious spiritual concepts are often reduced down to a simple diagram or three bullet points. Easy answers are given to all spiritual questions and issues, whether the questions and issues are simple *or* complex.

Again, those who are more Modern in their worldview don't see this approach to Christianity and church as problematic – indeed, they think it's just the way the faith and church are supposed to be. But those who are more Postmodern can spot it a mile away, and it not only doesn't appeal to them, they cannot relate to it at all. It doesn't resonate with the way they see and experience reality and life. The result: many of the churches that try so hard to be "relevant" end up being utterly *irrelevant* to Postmoderns.

*An Emerging Discontent*

The Postmodern issue – and the "emerging church," a term coined to refer to churches and Christians grappling with faith in a Postmodern culture, and of course used in the title of Dan Kimball's book – gave me a hook on which to hang my inchoate discontent with myself, Christianity, RidgePoint, the church at large, and my ministry. It gave me the promise of a new direction and purpose. I recognized myself in many of the Postmodern traits. I liked the idea of a more holistic approach to Christianity, not one that was primarily information-based. The idea of being less certain and simplistic about many areas of the faith also really resonated with me. Armed with this new information and inspiration, in the fall of 2004, I began conceiving of a way to maneuver all of this into a new ministry at RidgePoint. After working on it for several months, I issued my *Emerging Generations* proposal to the RidgePoint elders in December 2004.

My proposal mostly dealt with alternative methods on how to "do church" in a way that was more appealing to Postmoderns, that was more "emerging" in nature. Specifically, I proposed creating a separate worship service and/or "church within in a church" targeting Postmoderns. This meant worship gatherings that were more experiential, participatory, multisensory, and communal in nature, all emerging church buzzwords at the time. In focusing on methodology, I was mostly following Dan Kimball's lead. Although Kimball touched on some theological issues in his book, these were mostly just areas of emphasis (for example, helping the poor, the kingdom of God, being less dogmatic about "nonessential" issues, etc.). Kimball was not proposing any key doctrinal revisions; he was still thoroughly theologically conservative, and I was too. While I welcomed less certainty and simplicity on peripheral issues, I was still unmoving – at least consciously – on core conservative evangelical touchstones like atonement, hell, and Biblical inerrancy. It would not be long, though, before the inevitability of the larger theological implications of the Modern/Postmodern shift – and their resonance with many of my past issues, questions, and experiences – would become too great for me to ignore.

In the meantime, that fall I was beginning to consciously feel increasingly disconnected from RidgePoint and the version of the Christian faith I had embraced and propagated for so many years. How much of what I was thinking and feeling was *directly molded* by the writings of Kimball, McLaren and others – vs. *merely revealed* by these writings – is not clear. I suspect both were at play. Regardless, through their writing I was beginning to envision a church and faith setting that resonated more fully with this new way of thinking and being Christian, and this left RidgePoint and the ministries I was leading and participating in woefully deficient by comparison.

This became apparent at a fall '04 elder/leadership retreat, where I broke down sobbing during the worship singing. I remained very emotional throughout; every time I tried to sing, sorrow welled up from my depths again. Only by not singing could I gain some control of myself for the remainder of the worship time. Afterward, obviously the other leaders were concerned about me and asked if I was okay. Still emotional, I gave voice to it the only way I knew how at the time: *I was disappointed with the church* (at large, not just RidgePoint). I was disappointed with how inept the church often was at truly ministering to and inciting real transformation in people, our tendency to get distracted from what's really important and "major on the minors," people's lack of responsiveness and commitment to church leaders' efforts, our inability to convert people, etc.

There was certainly truth to that answer, and I mostly believed it at the time. But, it was an incomplete answer at best. Looking back, I knew in my gut that it was bigger than that. I was beginning to sense the disconnect between my role and ministry at RidgePoint and who I was becoming. It first occurred to me around that time that I would not likely be at RidgePoint long-term. At this point it didn't yet strike me as unavoidable, but looking back, I think I knew it was true deep down in my bones. I actually voiced this to an ex-staff member one evening in my church office that fall. Stating it out loud made it seem even more real and inevitable.

But also rising to my consciousness that fall was my overall disappointment with Christianity as a whole and with myself as a Christian. The disconnect wasn't just between me and my RidgePoint ministry role or how RidgePoint was "doing church." No, it was between what I allegedly believed and what I saw, felt and experienced in living my life. This was the ultimate source of the deep sorrow that I exhibited at the retreat. I could no longer pretend that everything was fine.

Kimball, McLaren and other authors gave life and words to the discontent and disconnect I was feeling. One of those other authors was Doug Pagitt, a pastor of an emerging church in Minneapolis. I could see my experience echoed in his life. He was on-staff at a contemporary evangelical seeker church, started experiencing a discontent and disconnect similar to what I was feeling, and ultimately left that church and started a faith community organized around the emerging thoughts, feelings, and passions of his evolving Christian faith. In his book *Reimagining Spiritual Formation*, he wrote these words that deeply resonated with me as I ended 2004 and entered 2005 (emphasis mine):

> "...a desire to be part of a community of faith that not only had a new way of functioning but also generated a different outcome. At that point, I had said, on more than one occasion, that I didn't think I would be able to stay Christian in any useful sense over the next 50 years if I continued with the expression of Christianity I was currently living – pretty disconcerting stuff for a pastor. This was not a crisis of faith in the typical sense; I never doubted God, Jesus, or the Christian faith. And yet I had a deep sense, which has actually grown deeper since, *that I needed to move into a Christianity that somehow fit better with the world I lived in...*"

> "My world wasn't crashing down. I wasn't at a moral crossroads; I hadn't hit rock bottom. *There was no big dramatic shift in my thinking but rather this lurking sense that there were levels of faith I knew nothing of and yet needed to enter if I was to remain a Christian at all. It was a feeling I couldn't shake, and*

*yet I also felt like I couldn't fully articulate what I needed. I just knew I needed something to change."*

Overall, like Pagitt, I had yet to experience what he called a "big dramatic shift in my thinking." Yet, I too had this "lurking sense" that "I needed something to change" that "I couldn't fully articulate" just yet, but would move me "into a Christianity that somehow fit better with the world I lived in." But, while not highly explicit in his book, Pagitt at least hinted at some dramatic shifts in thinking – theological shifts – that were more radical than what Kimball was proposing, or that I had been entertaining either. McLaren's *A New Kind of Christian* went just as far or farther, but I was yet to fully grasp the theological implications of this journey I was on. So, as I transitioned from 2004 to 2005, I was largely unaware that fully exploring and alleviating the disconnect between my faith and what I saw and experienced in living my everyday life would require me to make theological shifts that would have seemed unimaginable at the time.

# 4: 2005

The *Emerging Generations* proposal that I delivered to the RidgePoint elders in December 2004 received a generally tepid response. One elder was very enthusiastic about it, but to the others, it was just an unneeded distraction from all the other pressing issues they had to deal with, including keeping the existing ministry machine up and running. I was asked to do a fuller demographic analysis on the area around the church, including providing some information that was unobtainable unless costly research was conducted. Of course, there was no money to do this, and their intent in requesting further analysis was not explicitly stated but patently obvious: *we want to make this go away.*

I continued to hold out hope and periodically renew my push for an alternative postmodern service/community throughout part of 2005, prodded and encouraged by the one elder who had some passion for it. But, it increasingly took a back seat to my new project: trying to make sense of and answer my burgeoning intellectual and theological questions.

Generally speaking, most of my years at RidgePoint were *ministry* years, during which time I put intellectual and theological pursuits and questions on hold. RidgePoint and the seeker church movement in general were not particularly intellectually or theologically curious environments. The basics of the gospel were assumed, and the Bible was valuable primarily for its practicality and applicability to daily living, as well as proof-texting our assumed version of the gospel. Our job was not to bring up major intellectual or theological issues (unless, of course, it was to defend the faith and try to win over skeptics). No, our job was to communicate what we already knew in a relevant and compelling way to the seeker masses. And for me personally, I think I subconsciously – and perhaps even somewhat consciously – thought I had done enough exploring of intellectual issues earlier in my Christian life. And besides, I had largely arrived at the important answers. My focus was now on *action* and *doing*, not learning and exploring.

But by early 2005, I realized that over the past few years as I was preoccupied with ministry, I was in reality playing a theological version of an old game of my youth, Don't Spill the Beans. The game went like this: There was a pot that was already mostly filled with beans, and it was balanced precariously between two poles. Each player took turns placing beans in the pot, and with each bean added, the pot would wiggle a little more, becoming fuller and fuller and wobblier and more unbalanced. At some point, a player would place one bean too many in the pot, the pot would spill over, and the player who contributed that last pot-tipping bean would be the loser of the game.

Over my RidgePoint ministry years, when an intellectual or theological question invaded my mind, I attempted to deflect it with my conservative Christian defense shield – Bible verses or standard canned answers I had learned along the way – and I thought these questions were bouncing off and falling into oblivion. They were not. Rather, they were bouncing off the shield and collecting like beans in a pot in the back of my mind. By 2005, the pot was full, wobbly and unstable, and predictably and inevitably, it had to spill over. And spill it did in 2005, and when it did, it spilled forward, into the front of my mind. These intellectual and theological "beans" could no longer be ignored.

By early 2005, I was beginning to see beyond the methodological issues of Postmodern Christianity and church and starting to grasp some of the theological implications. The pot was beginning to spill, and I was beginning to get pretty confused theologically. I had all sorts of issues and questions racing through my brain, and I became intent on finding out more about these issues and questions. Consequently, 2005 was a year where I read voraciously. I would look at the footnotes and references of books I was reading for other authors and books that sounded helpful and interesting. While the books and authors I found gave me some hope that I would get past my theological bewilderment and eventually progress towards potential solutions, they mostly just raised more issues, causing even more beans to be added to an already-tipping pot. I was experiencing a rapid dismantling of my long-time faith package, what some philosophers – and some of the authors I was reading – called *deconstruction*.

*The Deconstruction*

I read two significant books in early 2005 that contributed to my theological deconstruction. One of these was *The Post-Evangelical* by Dave Tomlinson. Tomlinson offered several then-radical ideas. One, the very title, *Post-Evangelical*: someone who has moved on beyond, possibly even *out-grown*, conservative evangelical faith. A year, even six months earlier, I could not have imagined that such a person could exist. Now, as I read this book, I wondered if that was what I was, or at least rapidly becoming.

Two, Tomlinson's "church" met in a bar, during hours when the bar was open, and included few of the trappings of what I had always known as "church." No singing, no sermon, no praying. Mostly just discussion about a topic from the Bible with others who happened to frequent the bar. And they all drank beer while they had their discussion. I read in other books about more informal gatherings of Christians that included alcohol and had much less defined structure than any church-related gathering I'd ever been part of. I found this idea very appealing and freeing, but also terrifying.

But the most earth-shaking ideas for me at the time had to do with Tomlinson's questioning of some categories of traditional Christian morality. Certainly, alcohol was one of those. I had been a casual drinker for years, after giving it up entirely for a few years in my early 20s due to my fundamentalist fervor. I saw no conflict between my faith and drinking in my private life. But my casual drinking was kept very separate from my church life. Some leaders in our church did not drink at all, and some were vocally anti-drinking. Sometimes when I would order a beer at a restaurant, fear would rise up within me that someone from the church would see me. Early on, I had been taught that drinking was a key "stumbling block" issue, and so best to be avoided all together. Yet, I had seen and experienced the *magic* of alcohol – not in blatant drunkenness, but rather the sense of openness, realness and community that is often present when alcoholic beverages are enjoyed with others. And, I had experienced this most meaningfully with other *Christians*, just not in settings that were overtly or intentionally "spiritual," and certainly never in an "official" church setting. So, this was an area of tension for me, where my faith/church life didn't sync up fully with the rest of my life.

But Tomlinson went further: he questioned some of the distinctions between couples that were married and those that were living together. This opened up the issue of sex. Sex within conservative evangelicalism is very black and white. It is acceptable only within a marriage between a man and woman. Everything else is off-limits. (Scripture is rarely quoted supporting this view because there simply aren't any references to quote, at least explicitly and unequivocally. It can be argued, however, that the sexual mores are assumed, at least in the New Testament; Old Testament polygamy doesn't count!) While Tomlinson didn't go too far with this, he cracked the door to a more extensive questioning about this subject. I wasn't ready to go there yet, but I sensed that opening this crack further could unleash Pandora's Box, and it terrified and shook me.

The second significant book of early '05 was not a new one: I reread Brian McLaren's *A New Kind of Christian*, which I first read the previous fall, and this time it hit me like a ton of bricks. The book is semi-autobiographic fiction, with the main character, Dan Poole (at least partially based on McLaren himself) having a crisis of faith, which was intensified and had higher stakes because he was a pastor. In my first reading of the book, I was still mostly thinking methodology – how Postmodernism affects how we should "do church" and be Christian in this day and age. But now, in my recent state of theological rethinking and confusion, pastor Dan Poole's theological turmoil and professional predicament hit me full force, and I found myself resonating deeply with the character and with McLaren's writing in general.

*The Word of God?*

In *A New Kind of Christian*, McLaren wrote compellingly about another topic that would prove to be one of the most critical, pivotal, and challenging issues I would face: the origin, nature, meaning, and authority of the Bible. To conservative evangelicals, the Bible holds an exalted position. It is the literal Word of God. Yes, it was written *through* people, but the words are God's, and it is therefore inerrant and infallible, and the ultimate, even *sole*, source for doctrine and guidance. If you have a problem or question, the Bible has the answer. God reveals himself and his intentions for humanity through his perfect, inerrant, holy Word, the Bible. This is how I was taught to think about and use the Scriptures, and I embraced and propagated this view.

But while Tomlinson had also written about the Bible in his book, it was the two chapters in *A New Kind of Christian* that features dialogue between Dan Poole and his mentor Neo over the nature of Scripture that cogently raised the questions that I would wrestle with for several years. (Rob Bell's *Velvet Elvis*, which I read later in '05, was similarly influential in raising these kinds of questions.) Questions like, if the Bible is God's Word and contains "timeless truth," why does it seem to support so many things that we can no longer embrace – indeed, now declare as evil and abhorrent – like slavery, the subjugation of women, and genocide? When the Bible says God said to kill people and wipe out entire people groups: did he really, and if so, how does this sync up with a God that is also said to be slow to anger, full of compassion and love? For that matter, when it says that God spoke to people, was that an audible voice that anyone could have heard and that could have been recorded with today's audio recording technology, or was it something more internal, like a leading, prompting, or a "still small voice?" If the former, why does God's voice seem so much rarer today, and if the latter, why does it seem to be presented in the Bible as if it were the former? Furthermore, did some of the more incredible stories, like the creation account and the flood and the tower of Babel and Jonah and the whale, actually, historically happen, or are they better described as parables, allegories, poems or (dare we say it?) myths?

And, perhaps most perplexing for a book that is supposed to be an inerrant, clear revelation of God and his requirements for humanity: why does the Bible seem to contradict itself on so many subjects? Scriptural support can be found for extreme positions on both sides of many, many issues. Is God absolutely sovereign or do we have free will? Does God punish each person for their own individual sins, or for the sins of their parents, grandparents, great grandparents, and/or the leaders of their nation? Does God demand some sort of payment or sacrifice for sin – whether animals or Jesus the perfect human – or are we simply forgiven and accepted apart from any transaction? Are we saved totally by grace, or do works come into play? Is God changeless, or does he adapt and change his mind and actions according to human circumstances, decisions, actions, and supplication? Should we love and pray for our enemies, or exterminate them? Does everyone have equal access to God, or only those in an exclusive chosen group? Which is it? Would a book with such supposed authority really contain this kind of ambiguity? These kinds of questions would confound me – even haunt me – for a considerable period of time, and ultimately make me radically reconsider my view of and relationship with the Bible.

*Talking About It*

As I got into Spring '05, I was beginning to talk to a few people about my escalating theological deconstruction and confusion. I did this in fits and starts, and some attempts to disclose some of my theological questions were sometimes met with surprise, even shock, and left me feeling vulnerable and afraid of rejection… and honestly, also fearful of sliding down the "slippery slope" into heresy. In some cases, I still kept my difficulties disguised as primarily ecclesiological (i.e., how to "do church") and general spiritual angst. But regardless, the people in my life were beginning to become aware that all was not well with me. In a note I sent to the church elders in March '05, I shared this metaphor that I used with a number of people in the first half of '05 to describe my journey:

> A metaphor that I find myself often using to describe my journey is that of walking through a long dark tunnel. A few months ago, I could see only darkness as I looked ahead in the tunnel, and at times I felt very alone (though many times I could clearly feel God walking with me through the darkness, even guiding me). When I turned around and looked back, I could see the light from where I had been previously (representing the old way I viewed life, church, and relationship with and faith in Christ). It was at times very tempting to just turn around and run back to that previous place. It was familiar, and for many years, worked very well for me. But I didn't turn around and go back, because I remembered that I entered this tunnel for one

reason and one reason only: the "light" of the old place had ceased to be truly "light" for me – it had become small, constricting, dysfunctional, and ineffective. So, I have pressed on through the tunnel, scared as hell but doing my best to cling to God, my companion and guide.

As Easter approached, I was spiraling downward, swimming in confusion, anxiety and depression. So, on Good Friday 2005, I saw my family doctor, shared my mental and emotional state, and was put on an anti-depressant. I did my best to put on a happy face leading the RidgePoint Easter services that weekend, but it was excruciating; inside I was feeling intense pain and instability. There was some relief when the services were over, but overall, it was a hellish Easter.

That spring I also sought the professional help of a Christian counselor, who I saw perhaps a half dozen times during the second quarter of '05. At the time, given the confusion I felt and the general agony I was in, I wasn't sure it was all that helpful. But, he was very open and non-judgmental, and gave me a safe outlet to express my theological uncertainties and general anxiety as I went through my deconstruction.

A key thing that kept me going during this difficult time: I was beginning to find some others at RidgePoint that were having some similar questions and concerns as me. Sometimes this occurred as I apprehensively shared some of my struggles with someone and they related to them, having similar feelings and questions themselves. Sometimes others shared some of their concerns with me, and they were similar enough to mine that I felt safe divulging some of what I was experiencing. Two different people independently approached me that spring asking if I had heard of or read McLaren's *A New Kind of Christian*. All of these conversations helped me feel like I was not totally alone and gave me some hope. Some of these people would be conversation partners and fellow sojourners for years to come; indeed, some still are to this day.

*The "Emerging Conversation"*

That spring I also made my first venture outside RidgePoint to interact with others asking similar questions and thinking similar thoughts. In other words, I entered into what was called at the time the "*emerging* conversation" (you may have noticed that "emerging" was a popular word back then). In May, I traveled by myself to Nashville to attend the Emergent Convention, my first one, and the last one of its kind, as it turns out. Key authors I had been reading – Dan Kimball, Brian McLaren, Doug Pagitt, and others – were part of the Convention, leading breakout sessions. Earlier in the spring I asked the RidgePoint elders' permission to attend, and they graciously granted it to me (but, I'm sure they had no idea what is was all about, and if they had, they may have questioned it more).

The Emergent Convention was a bi-annual event held in different cities, co-sponsored by Emergent Village (an American-based international organization formed by those involved in the "emerging conversation," which also had local groups called Emergent cohorts), Zondervan, and Youth Specialties, and run concurrent with the National Pastors Conference. The National Pastors Conference was solidly conservative, and attracted a homogeneous group of mostly khakis-wearing white male pastors from suburban evangelical churches. By all appearances, it stuck closely to a conference formula of engaging, attractive, well-dressed young-to-middle-age speakers and worship leaders/singers, and slickly produced music, drama, video and multi-media, similar to all the conferences I had attended at Willow Creek over the previous years.

By contrast, Emergent Convention attendees and speakers were decidedly more diverse. Granted, mostly white and straight, but many women, various ages, and people from across the denominational and theological spectrum (in contrast to one of its sponsors: Zondervan was – and still is – a decidedly evangelical publisher). Generally, all of the attendees and speakers were dressed very casually (shorts, t-shirts, jeans, flip flops, etc.), and many had hipster tendencies (some were dyed-in-the-wool, full-blown hipsters). But, the keynote speaker at the general sessions was Phyllis Tickle, a 70-something Episcopalian woman! And there was no video, no multi-media, no drama, no worship band, and only limited music in general. It truly was more of a conversation than it was a traditional conference.

Just about everyone I talked to was in the same church and/or faith rethinking process as I was, so there was much common ground among the attendees, despite the diversity of theological and denominational backgrounds. And, there were fewer personal behavior taboos than in the evangelical culture. Attendees and speakers alike drank alcohol (one of the publishers held an event where they served beer!), some smoked, and some cursed. I found all of this generally refreshing, even invigorating and exciting (consistent with my desire to assuage the tension I experienced regarding drinking between my personal and church life). But, on some level, I felt a bit uneasy about it as well, as it was just *so* different from what I had experienced within the conservative evangelical subculture the previous two decades. With some trepidation, I shared this aspect of the convention with the RidgePoint elders in a Convention report I wrote for them upon returning.

One of the most interesting, memorable Convention experiences was the first seminar I attended, led by author Jim Henderson. Jim's gig was to interview "lost" people – people who generally claim to not be Christians – in front of a bunch of Christians. His stated goal was not converting the interviewees, but rather revealing reality and converting the Christians in the audience to treat non-Christians differently and with more respect. At the Convention seminar, Jim interviewed an attractive 30-ish year old woman who by just about everything she said appeared to be an active, involved, church-going follower of Christ, not a "lost" person. In fact, those in attendance began thinking to themselves: *Jim really messed up. He obviously didn't check her out carefully enough ahead of time to find out that she's really a Christian. He's got to be really embarrassed. This clearly isn't going as he had planned.* Then, just as we were all thinking this, she dropped the bombshell: she's gay. Most in that room would have said that being gay was an abomination and a sin (I had softened a bit on this issue by them, but if pressed, would have still affirmed the traditional, historic Christian view of homosexuality). Jim set us up big time, forcing us to deal with the tension of someone who claims a serious, meaningful faith in Christ, yet lives a lifestyle that the church has traditionally viewed as unequivocally contrary to Christian living. Jim didn't try to force any sort of "answer" in either direction to this tension; he simply exposed us to, using his words, "what's really going on out there." To what extent this experience influenced my multi-year evolution on the issue of homosexuality, I don't know. But, I do know this was the first time I was confronted with someone who claimed to be both Christian and gay, and it made a lasting impression on me.

*What the Hell?*

One of the hot (no pun intended) topics in hallway conversations at the Emergent Convention was Brian McLaren's recently released book *The Last Word and the Word After That*, which tackled the subject of hell. *The Last Word* was the third book in McLaren's *A New Kind of Christian* trilogy, continuing the ongoing story of pastor Dan Poole's faith evolution and dialogue with his mentor Neo. A few years later, Rob Bell would make a huge controversial splash with his own book on hell, *Love Wins*. But, *The Last Word* was that book for me, being my first encounter with the idea that maybe the issue of hell was not as cut and dried as I'd been taught or always assumed. It simply made Bell's 2011 book pretty anticlimactic for me.

Actually, I became aware of *The Last Word* about a month or so prior to attending the Emergent Convention, and knew that I would have to read it eventually. I put it off intentionally because I knew it would rock my world, a world that was already sufficiently rocked by everything else I was reading, thinking, feeling, and experiencing. (I would soon find out that McLaren's semi-fictional pastor Dan Poole had done the same thing with some books Neo had recommended to him!) I didn't need any more turmoil introduced into my life while still in the midst of the ministry season. But, arriving home from the Emergent Convention, with my interest piqued and the ministry season all but wrapped up, I quickly obtained the book and began devouring it.

Early in the narrative of the book, Neo tells Dan Poole that hell is "the issue that will change everything" for him. I remember reading that and, like many other things I had been reading, it simultaneously exciting and scaring the hell out of me (pun intended). But intuitively, I knew it was true. On many levels, I *wanted* everything to change. While the things that I had been reading the past six months or more gave me glimpses of something new and better, it mostly had just unsettled and disembedded me from my previous spiritual stability. But challenging the traditional notion of hell was very threatening. Hell was *absolutely integral and essential* to the eternity-focused theological system that I had been taught and had unquestionably embraced the past 25 years. Without hell, salvation and the gospel as I knew them were nonsensical and irrelevant. So, while in some ways I welcomed the change, in other ways I feared it would lead me fatally astray. However, I also ultimately felt I had no choice. I had to press on. I had to know.

I read and reread *The Last Word*, taking it all in. It did not answer all my questions, that's for sure. In fact, McLaren does not definitively state or land on a final, clear position on hell, and his book largely just raised more questions. But, it did give me the freedom and permission to feel like I could have questions about and explore beyond the traditional, conservative position on hell, specifically that everyone who does not explicitly accept Jesus Christ as Lord and Savior will automatically go there. And explore I did. Hell was one of my most researched and read about issues over the next year or so, as I eventually obtained and read about half a dozen of the books referenced in McLaren's footnotes. All the researching and reading, as well as much thinking, praying, and conversing with others, ultimately left me at considerable peace on the subject.

But the peace I ultimately arrived at on hell several years later is primarily the result of a revised image of God. In the book's introduction, McLaren wrote, "Ultimately, this book isn't about hell. It's about the character of God." Evangelical Christians always talk about the love of God. But just behind that is the threat of eternal conscious torment if you do not return that love. It's like children who live in the house of a father that they always feel like they have to say nice things about, but in secret, they know that dad keeps other children in the basement that he tortures. We have a name for that kind of person: a sociopath. The inconsistency of that image of God was simply unsustainable for me, and over time, I would eventually get to a healthier and more consistently loving version of God. And when that happens, hell kind of magically takes care of itself.

(Hell also becomes less relevant when your theology and your version of the gospel becomes more now-focused rather than afterlife-focused – more on that later.)

*I'm Goin' to Wichita...*

With all these various theological questions and issues spinning in my head, and coming off a ministry season where I was just trying to survive and make it through to the end in the midst of my theological turmoil, I entered the summer of '05 bewildered, perplexed, depressed, lonely and tired. A couple of days spent with one of my best friends seemed to be just what the doctor ordered. So, in early June, I went to Wichita to spend a few days with my friend Don.

We met Don and his wife Cathy at our church in Wichita in the mid-'80s shortly after both of us were married. Michelle and I were intentionally trying to get to know some other young Christian couples, so one Sunday we went to Sunday School class intending to invite whatever couple we sat next to over to our house to watch the upcoming Super Bowl. That couple was Don and Cathy. They had just moved from California to attend graduate school at Wichita State, and we quickly became fast, lifelong friends. Don and I could always have great fun *and* be very serious and vulnerable with one another, which was refreshing given the fun/serious friend split I had experienced during college. Don and Cathy moved back to California after they graduated, and since then we have looked for opportunities every year or two to spend some time together.

When we met in June, Don found me at near my worst. I articulated my questions and concerns about the Bible, truth, the church, and the evangelical faith in general. He shared some of those concerns, and we had great conversations, some of which stimulated him to reconsider portions of his faith, especially the role of the church and some of the theological emphases of the evangelical church (he went on to write a book about it). But on other issues – particularly the Bible and the question of "absolute truth" – he listened well and respectfully, but defended the traditional conservative positions on biblical inerrancy and truth. Overall, I think I alarmed him, if not by my theological issues, then certainly by the overall level of distress I was experiencing.

So, I came away from this time with Don encouraged in some ways by our common ground, and by just spending time with a friend who loves and accepts me regardless of my feelings, thoughts, and struggles. But in other ways, I was discouraged, because I sensed that we would have less in common going forward. We were both evolving theologically, but I intuitively knew that I was evolving more than he ever would. I think deep down I knew that I would eventually land in a place theologically that was different – perhaps *very* different – from his, and definitely different from the common theological space we had co-resided in all these years. And this saddened me; it was my first conscious feeling of loss in this faith journey.

*New Kind of Christians?*

In spite of feeling increasingly distant from some of my conservative friends and the evangelical faith and community in general, I had the growing sense that I was not alone in this roller-coaster journey of deconstructing and rebuilding my faith. But, up until the summer of '05, despite my time at the Emergent Convention, the vast majority of discussion I had engaged in about my budding theological questions had been individual, one-on-one conversations with a few people at RidgePoint. However, through those individual contacts, I now had a half dozen or so with whom I was now having some level of ongoing dialogue on these issues. So, I took a somewhat bold step in June '05: I formed a short-term group that would meet several times over the summer, and we would read and discuss Brian McLaren's *A New Kind of Christian.*

The discussions that summer with this group of people were interesting and invigorating for me. We met at the RidgePoint church building, and I'll admit that it felt somewhat dangerous to be talking about the things we were talking about there. Not everyone agreed with everything McLaren wrote, and in fact one of those in the group would become an outspoken critic of the book, McLaren, and the ideas and questions he raised, retreating to a very conservative, non-questioning faith. Because she was one of the founders of RidgePoint, very outspoken and influential, and good friends with other leaders and staff members, her dissent from the group would in due course prove detrimental to the spread of these ideas at RidgePoint. But regardless, what that group did was form a small community of like-minded people, some of whom are to this day still in community with one another.

In fact, Michelle and I were rapidly becoming very close, indeed best friends, with a couple in that group, Dan and Lana. As the summer discussion group was wrapping up, despite the one person's negative reaction to the book, I came up with an even crazier idea: forming an official RidgePoint small group (called a Life Group) around *A New Kind of Christian* and the ideas and questions expressed in it. And we recruited Dan and Lana to start and co-lead it with us, starting in September 2005. To promote the group and try to attract the right kind of members (i.e., members who would be open and not immediately react against it), I promoted the topic of the group as "exploring fresh new ways of being a Christian in 21st century America," to explore the question "What does it mean to be a follower of Jesus Christ, both individually and collectively, in our evolving American cultural context?" While I hinted at implications for our Christian beliefs, it was more positioned around how we express, talk about, and live out our faith, and this attracted a fairly diverse group of reasonably open-minded RidgePoint attendees.

Even more than the summer discussion group, this group became very life-giving for me. Even though I was a staff member, I felt safe with this group, safe to explore not just new ways to express our faith, but new ways to think about it, new ways to believe. Not that everyone agreed with me, McLaren, or one another. But we were all open to considering and talking about new and different ideas, and we respected one another's opinions and gave freedom to one another to explore and discuss implications to both practices *and* theology. Through the group, I found more people who, at least on some level, could relate to some of the thoughts and questions I was having about my faith. The group would prove to be a very important source of community and support for me during the events of the coming months.

Meanwhile, I continued to read avidly. A couple of the books I read around this time that resonated with me and advanced my thinking:

- *A Churchless Faith*, by Alan Jamieson. Jamieson personally interviewed hundreds of people who left the evangelical church, and classified them into groups according to the nature of their faith post-church. I saw myself in a couple of these typologies (Reflective Exiles and Transitional Explorers) who had jettisoned substantial portions of their previous "faith package" (a Jamieson phrase for a particular set of doctrines, beliefs, and practices) and were trying to find a way forward outside of the traditional conservative evangelical church. Except, of course, I had not left the church... at least not yet. But, it helped me place myself and my experience in a broader context, and reinforced that I was not alone in my struggles.

- *Velvet Elvis*, by Rob Bell. I had heard of Bell's *Nooma* videos, but this was my first direct experience with his thinking and writing. He had (has) a unique way of writing and communicating in general, but the issues he was writing about pushed all my buttons. His chapter on the Bible was the best articulation of my emerging view of Scripture that I had read to that point, and I actually made a copy of the chapter and distributed it to the RidgePoint elders, representing it as the best-written version of how I was coming to view the Bible. This book also became the book we read and discussed after *A New Kind of Christian* in our newly formed Life Group.

*Reassessing My Calling*

As I transitioned from summer to fall, through all my reading, thinking, and wrestling, and my newfound discussion partners, I found myself starting to find my sea legs theologically. Or, at least I was able to better articulate my key issues and questions, and being able to do this helped me feel a bit less theologically unstable than in the spring and early summer. But, along with that came a growing suspicion that my theology was evolving beyond what would be acceptable at RidgePoint, especially for a leader, and especially for a staff member.

So, it seemed like the right time to be more transparent with the RidgePoint elders about my situation. In September I wrote a seven-page treatise titled *Reassessing My Calling*, outlining the theological, ecclesiological, and financial issues pressing down on me and causing me to question my staff and leadership role at RidgePoint. I had two long, excruciating meetings with the elders during September and October 2005 where in painstaking detail we pored over my treatise and the issues outlined within. In some ways, I felt affirmed by these meetings. Although I brought up some very controversial theological topics – such as my evolving views of the Bible, hell and homosexuality – I explicitly asked the elders if they still viewed me as qualified for a staff and leadership position at RidgePoint given my evolving views. They affirmed my qualification, and that my evolving views did not disqualify me from RidgePoint ministry (although the topics clearly made some elders pretty uncomfortable). In other ways, it seemed like I was being put through the ringer, and being subjected to a trial on my orthodoxy. But, to be fair, I was the one driving these meetings – I'm sure the elders would have loved to avoid them if they could have.

Through all this, as the theological darkness descended a bit, and my ability to articulate new theological and methodological ideas grew, the idea of pastoring an emerging-type church continued to be attractive. I brought it up repeatedly in my interactions with the elders in the fall of '05. I put forward ideas of forming a steering committee or core team to investigate the possibility of planting a RidgePoint-sponsored church to reach Postmoderns, or at least a separate alternative service within RidgePoint that I would lead and pastor. As with my *Emerging Generations* proposal almost a year earlier, the response was lukewarm at best. So, while in my meetings with the elders they ostensibly affirmed my future as a RidgePoint staff member and leader, it was becoming more and more clear that that was within the current theological and methodological framework of the church, not in any sort of ministry offshoot that I could tailor to my increasingly post-evangelical leanings.

All of this was now producing a career crisis. My dilemma was this: I had now been in professional ministry for over six years, and I found myself unable to imagine a future outside of that. So, I began researching some options. In doing so, unfortunately, I found that a) ministry jobs for those without an advanced ministry/theological education were limited, and b) regardless, none of them paid any more than I was making at RidgePoint – in fact, I might even have to take a pay cut to go somewhere else (more on the money side of things shortly). Moreover, where would I go? Once my background (no formal theological training or education) and theology (TBD, but evolving somewhere between conservative evangelical and something else) were considered, I had few, if any, real options.

So, I had another idea: what if I went to seminary, to give myself space to truly study and form new theological convictions, as well as build up my credentials to parlay into a new ministry position elsewhere? I considered this for a couple of weeks and did some online research about various seminary options, and then sprung the idea on Michelle over dinner one night that fall at our favorite restaurant J. Gilbert's. She did *not* react favorably to it (to say the least), and the conversation we had that night and in the weeks that followed made me more aware of a developing issue: the growing distance between what I wanted (or at least what I *thought* I wanted) and what Michelle and our family needed.

The most obvious sign was our family finances. Our kids were growing into teenagers who needed braces and cars, and we were getting more and more financially strapped. In the first few years of working at RidgePoint, I had done a bit of marketing research consulting on the side to supplement my meager ministry income, but that had completely dried up by early 2005. Michelle had been cleaning houses since I first went on-staff at RidgePoint over six years earlier, and had built her business up over time, but in light of my reduced income and the increased financial demand of growing kids, it wasn't enough. She added a part time job that summer, working 20 hours a week in addition to keeping her house-cleaning business going.

Additionally, Michelle had always been very involved in our kids' schools, volunteering and heading up committees and events, doing in-class tutoring, giving rides home to other kids who didn't have a parent to pick them, etc. This was her passion, but the workload associated with holding down two jobs was squeezing that out. To mix metaphors, she was burning the candle at both ends trying to keep all the balls in the air, and she was getting stressed and exhausted.

Added to that, of course, was all I was going through in my faith deconstruction. Throughout 2005, as I was distracted rethinking so much of my faith and theology, Michelle was just trying to keep the house and family running. I certainly shared with her what was going on with me, but in limited doses. I didn't want to completely freak her out, so I held back many times, except when I felt it was really critical, and certainly when I was experiencing obvious depression and anxiety. So, while Michelle tried to be a listening ear and a strong support to me – which she never failed to be throughout my entire deconstruction – she was obviously worried about me. She also was trying to at least somewhat shelter the kids from my emotional state, not wanting to upset them or have them worrying too much about me. All of this, in addition to the financial struggles, was weighing on her when I told her I was thinking of going to seminary. She simply recognized it right away as being untenable for our family, and not long after I was thankful that she had.

Looking back on it now, of course, I can see what a bad idea seminary was. While I might have been able to do something online or locally, the seminaries that really interested me were not in Kansas City, so would have involved uprooting our family, something that Michelle absolutely did not want, and truly neither did I. And of course, all options would have cost a lot of money that we simply did not have. Ultimately, the seminary idea was a fantasy I had concocted as a solution to my unsustainable career predicament, much like the fantasy of pastoring a new emerging-type church, which I was absolutely not in a good spot to lead, either theologically or emotionally.

So, as the fall wore on, with the seminary idea fully dead, the elders' tepid response to anything related to an alternative church or service, our family dynamic out of sync, and our financial issues deepening, I reconsidered whether paid ministry was really truly my future. In November, I reached out to a former marketing research colleague, and began a consulting arrangement with a marketing research firm in December. The agreement had me working a limited amount of time per week for the marketing research firm, while maintaining my full-time position at RidgePoint. I got this approved with the elders, and looking back, it was probably clear to both them and me that this was the beginning of the end of my time as a RidgePoint leader and staff member.

To state the obvious, a lot happened in 2005. I entered the year as a fully committed RidgePoint leader and staff member, and intrigued and excited by the possibilities of my burgeoning quest for a more Postmodern expression of faith and ministry. I wrapped up the year changed theologically, and by taking a decidedly large and definitive step towards exiting full time paid ministry altogether, that would continue to take its natural course the following year.

# 5: 2006

In the early part of 2006, my new part-time marketing research consulting job proved to be a useful distraction from my theological angst. I was rusty as far as marketing research was concerned, but excited to be doing something new, and to not have all my professional eggs in the ministry basket. Balancing a full-time ministry job with a part-time consulting gig was challenging some weeks. But, the areas I was responsible for at RidgePoint did not discernably suffer, because by that point we had hired a part-time person to help with Creative Arts, and I had delegated quite a bit more to volunteers. This helped me not have to burn the candle at both ends, and also not be as constantly and relentlessly confronted by RidgePoint's ministry and theology that were increasingly in conflict with my evolving ecclesiological and theological views.

*On My Way Out*

As the end of February neared, the elders reached out to me to check in, both on how my marketing research consulting gig was going in relation to my role at RidgePoint, and on where I stood in terms of my calling reassessment. In response, I wrote them a very positive yet very vague note, saying pretty much nothing of substance. But, it was becoming clearer and clearer in my mind throughout the winter and early spring what was going to happen: at some point in the reasonably near future, I was going to resign from the staff of RidgePoint.

I was conversing about all of this with four friends that I referred to at the time as my "D" team, as all had a first or last name that began with "D." I sent them an email in early April to inform them of my impending decision to resign from RidgePoint, outlining the theological, ecclesiological, and family changes driving my decision, and inviting them to point out any flaws in the decision itself or the reasoning behind it. With none of the "D" team throwing up any red flags, in early May I informed pastor Brad, the staff, and the elders of my decision to resign.

When I told Brad, the news didn't land with him initially, and he, rather ironically, immediately started talking about the possibility of something I had tried to push through for over a year: leadership of a RidgePoint church plant. But it was simply too late; I was done. I cut off any talk of continued employment very quickly, and he and the other leaders all ultimately accepted the news graciously.

On May 21, I stood up in both Sunday services and announced that I would be transitioning off the RidgePoint staff sometime during the second half of 2006. I said all the right things to try make the news as palatable and uncontroversial as possible. I made it clear that my family and I would not be leaving RidgePoint, but would remain an active part of the church. I also explicitly stated that I was not leaving staff because anything bad or wrong had happened on my part or the part of anyone else on-staff or in leadership, nor was I leaving because I was mad about anything. While I said there were "numerous factors that were taken into consideration in making this decision," I certainly did not go public with my theological and ecclesiological evolution and angst; I kept things very vague, positive, and related to following "God's leading" – a conversation-stopping trump card to which no counter argument can be effectively made. While there were many who were surprised by the news, and certainly some that expressed concern about what my leaving said about the church and its leadership, most seemed to take the news well.

I lame-ducked it at RidgePoint throughout the summer of '06 while I looked for a job. I found one rather quickly: a full-time position with the marketing research company I was consulting for, which I agreed to start in mid-August (and I am still working for that company to this day). In the meantime, I handed more and more of my previous ministry responsibilities to others in light of my looming staff departure.

Pastor Brad took an extended time off during that summer, and agreed to let me plan and lead my first ever sermon series. I entitled it "God's Country: Living in the Kingdom of God," inspired by a new book my Life Group and I were reading and discussing that summer: Brian McLaren's *The Secret Message of Jesus*. I was increasingly anchoring my evolving theology and ecclesiology on Jesus's message of the kingdom of God in the gospels, especially the here-and-now kingdom-on-earth aspect. This series gave me not only a chance to explore that further, but to try to articulate it in a concise and persuasive form to others. While I only personally delivered two of the sermons, I planned the content, recruited and organized the other speakers, and arranged a resource table that included types of books that were never before and have never since been offered at RidgePoint, including the McLaren book. While the experience was mostly fulfilling to me, and I received positive reviews of my messages, the books didn't exactly fly off the resource table, and the whole experience solidified my sense that I was just in a different place theologically now than most folks at RidgePoint. It was definitely time for me to become more removed from the day-to-day inner workings and leadership of the church.

*Untethered from Professional Ministry*

I officially left staff in mid-August and started my full-time marketing research job. However, it took longer to truly transition out of visual and actual leadership. As the ministry season cranked up for the fall, I was still in charge of RidgePoint's budgeting process for the coming year, and I continued to lead worship most Sundays. Also, after strongly considering ending our Life Group in the summer, we ultimately decided to re-up for the fall. Some transitioned out of the Life Group from the previous year, but we promoted it similarly to a year earlier, titling it *A New Kind of Life Group* (get it?), and got 24 adults to sign up! That proved to be too many – we had difficulty finding a good space to hold the meetings, and it was just too hard to have meaningful discussions with that many people. But, more than that, many of the new members were simply not ready for the kind of discussion topics some of us, who had been thinking about and discussing these things for over a year, wanted to engage in.

The Life Group, which had been so life-giving and sustaining the year before, was now full of people completely new to these ideas. From the very first meeting, I knew leading this group was going to be more difficult than the previous year's group, and preparing for and leading it only got more draining as the fall wore on. And, in the midst of trying to lead the group, I was beginning to really struggle again theologically. I didn't realize it fully yet, but being untethered from a staff leadership position would free me to begin a line of questioning that previously had seemed off-limits, and still terrified me. This is expressed in this journal entry from late September, which includes the germ of an idea that ultimately became what you're reading now (I should note here that you will see more journals entries from here on out; I journaled previous to this, but lost all of them in a hard drive crash a month earlier):

> I'm really struggling spiritually and theologically. Every once in a while, I still just seem to go through these times where I can't put it all together and nothing makes sense. In those times, I long for the old days of unreflected-upon certainty, when I had the Christian faith all figured out and nailed down to a manageable list of propositions. Damn Emergent! Although they really just articulated what I had been beginning to feel in recent years.

> This all started now a little over two years ago with the reading of Dan Kimball's *The Emerging Church*. As I was soon to find out, a mild introduction indeed. It was two years ago this month that I first read McLaren's *A New Kind of Christian*, which ultimately changed my world. Since then, I have read probably 40-50 books, all challenging on various levels what I have spent the previous 25 years learning and believing. In doing so, I have replaced some of my long-held beliefs with new ones, at least on a provisional basis. But I have yet to consistently get to the point of certainty and confidence that I had before – and may never get there. I have these periods where I wonder if any of it is true. I never doubt that God exists and is real, and has been real to me. But, I do begin to doubt some of the specific doctrines and underpinnings – key foundational ones – of the Christian faith. For instance, is Jesus really the ONLY way to God, or perhaps just the best, most complete way? It's always

been very black and white in the past: if you reject Jesus, even reject him as the only way, then you have rejected God and are in fatal error. I don't think I can see it as that black and white any more. Is it truly authentically Christian to believe that Jesus was in some way God come to earth and the best representation of God we've ever had without throwing out all other religions altogether, all other attempts by man to capture this mystery that is the divine?

Lots of questions. I'm not sure who to dialog with about all of this. The Kansas City area Emergent Cohort is beginning to have monthly meetings now, and had one last night. I didn't go. I had an excuse, but honestly didn't feel like it either. I'm not sure I can have some of these deeper conversations with RidgePoint folks, when I'm looked at as the leader (especially true of our Life Group). Should I be looking for people outside of RidgePoint? If so, it would seem like the Cohort would be the place to look. But, I also wonder if a smaller group of folks could/should meet regularly to discuss some of the bigger theological issues like the Bible, the atonement, and hell. Could/should I pull that together? I guess I feel like dealing with all of this in isolation is not ideal. I also know that I tend to process things better when I write. I've considered starting to do that, starting to compose a personal manifesto, so to speak.

These times like I'm in now don't come along as often as they used to, but when they do, it's tough. It feels like I'm losing my faith. God, don't let that happen. But also don't let me hang on to things that are just not true, or let me do so just for comfort's sake. I want to know the truth. If that means in some way going back to where I came from, lead me there. But admittedly, that seems impossible now. I've gone too far, and it would be intellectually dishonest. Help me, Lord.

Around that time, I also began reading a book I had been aware for a while, but had intentionally put off reading until after I left the RidgePoint staff: *The Heart of Christianity* by Marcus Borg. Borg was easily the most liberal of the authors I'd read so far, and I knew the book had the potential to be another earth-shattering experience for me. All the other authors I had been reading the past two years were either recently evolving evangelicals or post-evangelicals. In both cases, they started with a conservative evangelical background and framework, experienced deconstruction, and were now writing about what theology and faith could look like post-deconstruction. Borg was a Christian, but decidedly not evangelical, then or ever. So, he had fewer shackles on his theology than the other authors I'd read, and as such introduced me to some new ideas that I hadn't dared to consider yet.

For example, new to me in Borg's writing was the idea that the historicity of some of the events in Jesus's life don't really matter – for instance, many of the miracles, or Jesus's literal virgin birth or bodily resurrection – what matters is what they *mean*, not whether they literally happened. Now I had previously encountered the idea that some of the events of the Old Testament, particularly the creation, the Garden of Eden, and other parts from Genesis, did not literally happen as they were written, and might be more akin to poetry or allegory than recorded historical fact. Further, I had largely embraced that notion and was becoming increasingly comfortable with it. But, saying that some of the events in Jesus's life as recorded in the four gospels may not have actually, literally happened in the way I had been taught to understand and believe, was alarming to me, and got to the very core of Christianity itself. I was holding fast to the idea that at least the accounts of Jesus were historically accurate, and certainly his birth, death and bodily resurrection. I didn't exactly know what to do with any of this yet; I had other burgeoning questions that were occupying my mind.

One of those questions was the exclusivity of the Christian faith, mentioned earlier in my September journal entry. Borg was unapologetically pluralist, not believing that Christianity was the only way to encounter and experience the divine. Yet at the same time, he held that Jesus and the Bible were absolutely central and essential to being Christian. While this confused me, it also gave me some glimpse of eventually coming to some resolution on an issue that continued to vex me for months to come.

But, on the whole, Borg's writing resonated with me deeply, and was consistent with pretty much everything I had been thinking about and reading. In particular, his thoughts about the Bible and atonement were very interesting and thought provoking to me. While I wasn't yet ready to go as far as he had, it was refreshing to hear someone talk about these topics with an ease and freedom that comes from not having the restraints of conservative evangelicalism holding you back. But, while Borg would ultimately be a key influence in my journey in the coming years – particularly *The Heart of Christianity* – reading him that first time that fall exacerbated my downward spiral.

However, in the midst of it all, there were still small encouraging signs that fall. RidgePoint decided to offer a series of single-session book discussion groups, and I led one on – what else? – Brian McLaren's *A New Kind of Christian*. A RidgePoint-sponsored discussion of this book would have been simply unimaginable a year earlier. Eighteen people attended, and the discussion was engaging and vibrant. Additionally, around this same time, I had some email interaction with one of the more conservative elders, who told me that I had significantly affected his thinking on some things.

*Hello Darkness My Old (and New) Friend*

Still, overall, the darkness deepened as I ended the year. I was struggling intensely, the Life Group was not going well, and I felt exhausted and unequipped to continue leading it. Michelle and I talked with Dan and Lana in late November and agreed it was time to end the Life Group. So as December rolled around, I was feeling increasingly dark and confused. Some journal entries from December:

> *December 4, 2006*
>
> Last week was a tough week for me. I had the toughest week spiritually that I'd had in a while. Many doubts, many questions; BIG questions, like is any of this stuff real. I hate having that level of questions. But in some cases, the more I learn about world history and other ancient beliefs the less unique Christianity becomes, and the less I can accept its exclusivist claims. But I desperately want to continue to be a Christian, because if I'm honest, I know deep down that I have experienced and encountered the living God of the universe through Jesus. Is that the only way people can do that? And if it's not, does that necessarily invalidate Christianity? I don't think so, at least I hope not. But those who would say so would tend to be much more liberal theologically and not believe

many other things that I guess I hope to still believe – the literal resurrection, for example. I don't know. Lord, I want to believe; help me with my unbelief.

*December 11, 2006*

Still struggling. Not that there haven't been some bright spots and good moments recently, but overall I'd say I'm definitely in a down period. And it largely comes down to this: on some level, I think I am in mourning over the loss of my old life. A life characterized by certainty and a wider camaraderie with those who shared it. Sure, we may have differed on how certain things should be done at church or how certain things should be expressed, and even about a few "truths" (the role of baptism comes to mind), but we shared this view of the world where Christianity was absolutely true and everything else was absolutely false. That way of life is gone for me. I don't know exactly what its replacement is, and who I will ultimately find commonality with in this new world order, but that's what I guess I'm in search of: people who have left that old world as well and are in search of a new one and people to travel there with. I have a few at RidgePoint, but I'm their leader, and I really feel like I need to be led on this journey, at least at some level.

*December 18, 2006*

I am still struggling spiritually. Actually, I'm not sure "spiritually" is a completely accurate way to say it – I am still praying and in conversation with God. It's more that I'm struggling with some of the logical and internal consistencies of traditional Christianity. It comes down to this:

1.  With all I know, can I really still hold to the exclusivism of Christianity? And, by letting go of that, can I still be truly Christian?

2.  How does Jesus's death figure into the story? In much of traditional Christianity, that IS the story. I don't buy that anymore – the traditional way of understanding his death just doesn't make sense to me anymore in light of

his life, resurrection, and of all Jewish history before. But, I am having a hard time coming up with a cogent alternative.

O God, please help me with these things. Guide me to truth, clarification, and understanding. Where ambiguity is inevitable, let me accept that. Where clarity is possibly, let me find it. Don't let me lose my faith in you in the process.

So, while most of the year was a bit of a break in my faith deconstruction while I dealt with what I was going to do professionally, I ended 2006 right back in the thick of it, absolutely reeling with a deepening sense of despair and loss. I felt alone and rudderless, and other than my family, on the brink of losing everything I had based my adult life on: my faith, my faith community, and I don't think it's hyperbolic to say, my God. I was seeking something or someone to help me gain my footing, and some sense of stability and belonging again.

# 6: 2007

The calendar said it was a new year, full of new possibilities and such, but as 2006 transitioned to 2007, I found myself in exactly the same place: a fog of confusion and escalating despair. I sensed that if I was going to ever get beyond this disorientation and darkness, I needed to do something different from what I had been doing up to that point. So, in early January I made a list of things that I needed to do, and sooner than later:

- *Distance myself more from RidgePoint.* By this time, taking part in, or even attending, the Sunday services sent me into a tailspin nearly every time. Everything about the services – the songs, the God-talk from fellow attendees, the theology, content and length of the sermons – was triggering to me. I not only needed to abdicate all my leadership responsibilities at RidgePoint, I also simply needed to be there less often.

- *Explore some other avenues spiritually.* I thought about possibly attending another church part-time, but I wasn't sure which one.

- *Find some regular traveling companions/conversation partners* in my spiritual journey now that my Life Group had ended and I was distancing myself from RidgePoint. I wasn't exactly sure who that was in early January, but I knew I needed it desperately.

- *Find a spiritual director*, someone who was skilled and practiced in the art of listening, asking questions, and simply walking alongside people in their spiritual journeys – especially trying and circuitous ones like mine. I knew my friend Jim, a youth minister at another church who was on a similar path as mine, had seen a spiritual director, so I determined to talk to him about this.

- *Expand my reading to authors outside of emerging church circles*, to include stuff that at one time I would have considered not only too liberal, but downright heretical.

These intentions, and my follow-through on them in the coming weeks, would make the month of January 2007 perhaps the most pivotal time in my quest for some sort of peace and equilibrium.

*Less Church / Church-less?*

First, I quit leading worship at RidgePoint. I continued to periodically play the guitar during services, but I did not lead, rather staying back with the band and out of the spotlight. And, I mostly quit attending when I wasn't playing. In those off weeks, sometimes I would just stay home. Other times, I would visit other churches. Michelle and the kids did not go with me, they continued to attend RidgePoint weekly. Michelle knew I was in crisis, and that attending RidgePoint was emotionally triggering to me, so she graciously gave me the freedom to explore some other church settings.

I started with two prominent churches in the area that I knew were less conservative than RidgePoint, one of which was Jacob's Well. It met in a cool old church building in midtown Kansas City, and was full of young hip adults, the very folks that Dan Kimball wrote were largely missing from churches in *The Emerging Church*. As such, Jacob's Well was often considered a prominent example nationally of a successful and thriving emerging church. I found much of what they were doing attractive, but also found that they were more conservative theologically than I had already become. The hipster vibe disguised a theology that, while certainly more generous than what I was coming from, was still firmly evangelical. This was a disappointment to me, as I think I was hoping Jacob's Well would end up being my part-time – maybe eventually full-time – church (although it would have been a considerable drive from my home in the suburbs).

The other one was Church of the Resurrection (known locally as COR), a United Methodist megachurch. They had a four-week series on the book of Revelation that I decided to attend in full (they had a Saturday night service and multiple Sunday morning services that I could attend even on the weeks I went to RidgePoint). Similar to Jacob's Well, I liked a lot of what the church was doing, and the theology was much more moderate than what I was coming from. The series on Revelation was thoughtful and intellectual, a far cry from the fear mongering Left Behind/Late Great Planet Earth-esque messages I'd encountered previously in churches and parachurch groups. But again, it didn't take long to realize that they were more conservative theologically than I already was – they had the congregation recite a version of the sinner's prayer the last two weeks of the Revelation series, for God's sake! – and again, this was disappointing to me.

I also visited an unambiguously liberal church, Saint Andrew's Christian Church. Unlike RidgePoint, which was an *independent* Christian church, Saint Andrew's was a Disciples of Christ church, one of the more liberal denominations in the United States, and practically anathema to a conservative independent Christian church like RidgePoint.

Saint Andrew's was unapologetically LGBTQ welcoming and affirming. While I was okay with that in theory, the number of gay couples in the service I visited made me uncomfortable. To state the obvious, I had never encountered that in a church service before, and it brought to the surface that I indeed still held the belief that "God's best design" for all people was heterosexuality. Gay people were absolutely accepted by God and certainly not going to hell (not that I still believed in a literal hell by then), and I wouldn't have even called homosexuality a sin at that point. However, ultimately, deep down I still felt gay people were coming up short of God's best for their lives. That was okay; I knew I was coming up short of God's best in one or more areas of my life too. But, as I saw full inclusion in practice, I realized I was not there yet.

I am somewhat ashamed to say all of that now, but that is honestly where I was in 2007. Even though it doesn't seem that long ago, it was a fundamentally different time. This was eight years before same-sex marriage became legal in the United States, and even the vast majority of progressive politicians (including progressive hero Barack Obama) still opposed gay marriage, as did all but the most liberal of churches and theologians. My views on all of this would change shortly as my theology continued to evolve, and as I began encountering more gay people in my life.

Otherwise, like with Jacob's Well and COR, there were things I liked about Saint Andrew's. They were friendly, open and inclusive (albeit a bit too inclusive for where I was at that time). The theology was definitely closer to what I was rapidly evolving to, but it went a little too far for me then. Additionally, I had been involved in contemporary evangelical church services for so long that some of the mainline practices turned me off a bit. I think I was still looking for some of the trappings of a contemporary evangelical church service (which were present at both Jacob's Well and COR), despite the fact that many aspects of those services, including contemporary evangelical worship music, had ceased to be meaningful to me, and in fact could be triggering. (I know, I sound very fickle, but because I was drifting between two theological worlds at that time, I was never going to find something that fully fit.) Bottom line: While I really, *really* wanted to like Saint Andrew's, there were too many things that didn't quite resonate with me.

So, in early 2007, it was three-strikes-and-you're-out on finding a church where I could feel more at home. I had visited three churches that I had high hopes of feeling like I could be a part of, but I didn't quite fit in any of them. And, I certainly didn't fit any longer at RidgePoint. This left me feeling homeless and alone.

Around this same time, as I experienced life after leaving a church staff position five months earlier, and as I considered what life was becoming as I became less involved in a church than I had my entire adult life, I came across a book I'd heard about months back: *Leaving Church* by Barbara Brown Taylor. She was an Episcopal priest for about 20 years, and then, as she put it, left it to save her faith. Her experience was very much like mine: questions and doubt began to creep in towards the end of her time in ministry, but she could largely push it back. However, once she left the ministry, she no longer could; the dam broke and the questions flooded in, but now she had the time and freedom to openly explore them. Reading all of this encouraged me, because of course I could relate to it so much, but it also disturbed me because of how thoroughly it dislocated her from her previous version of faith. And now that I was untethered from church leadership – and in many ways, from a church, period – I was feeling very dislocated indeed.

*If Not Church… What?*

I continued to pursue other spiritual environments where I thought I could find help and community fitting my current disoriented condition. In early January, I scheduled lunch with my friend Jim. We met at Barley's Brewhaus, a place that had 100 taps of beer, which was more than any other place I'd seen up to that point (while less unique now than then, it's *still* a lot of taps). He introduced me to Barley's Mug Club, where you paid a small annual fee, got your own personal, special mug that you drank from every time you came, and discounted beer for the year. What a deal! He also referred me to a spiritual director he had seen named Craig who ran an organization called Rhythm of Grace, which offered various programs and services for spiritual formation.

I met with Craig for lunch in mid-January. I liked him personally, and I liked his focus on ancient/classic spiritual practices. While he was certainly open to us meeting regularly one-on-one, he really encouraged me to sign on for his yearlong program called Pilgrim's Process, which included four weekend retreats at Conception Abbey about two hours north of Kansas City, supplemented by one-on-one sessions with Craig in-between. I initially was very torn about whether I wanted to do this or not. On one hand, it cost $1,000 for the year, and four weekends away, which seemed like a lot of money and time back then with everything involved with having a family full of teenagers. And, I feared that it would feel a lot like some of the churches I was investigating: full of generous promise and intrigue on the outside, but largely same-old-same-old evangelical theology and people on the inside. But, the immersive experience and the classic spiritual practices focus were very attractive to me. I didn't have long to deliberate, because the first retreat was coming up just two weeks from that initial meeting. My gut told me I should do it, and Michelle thought I should do it too, so I did. I definitely perceived risk in doing it, but ultimately, I was drowning, searching for any nearby life raft, and this seemed like one I should grab hold of and see if it could help me float.

*A Pilgrim Finally Finds a Process*

The first Pilgrim's Process retreat confirmed some of my fears. The theology was basically evangelical (maybe evangelical-light would be a better description; evangelical, but not stridently so). So were all the other attendees; none were questioning evangelicalism as a whole like I was. While that made me somewhat uncomfortable at times, overall the first retreat resonated with me deeply, because the framework for the entire spiritual formation program was something to which I'd recently become exposed: *the stages of faith.*

Many varied authors have written about the stages of faith, including James Fowler, Brian McLaren, and Richard Rohr. They vary in the number of faith stages; Fowler uses six, McLaren four, and Rohr two (first and second halves of life). But the basic idea and progression is essentially the same, and I could see it very clearly in my life. First, you have an *awakening*, an initial awareness of the divine, which can include some sort of overt conversion to faith. Then, there's *learning and belonging*, were you belong to a group that believes and values the same things as you do, and you learn the doctrine and behaviors to which you should adhere as a member of that group. Next, you enter some sort of *ministry* – not professional ministry, but a moving outward into service to others, giving back as it were.

If you go back and review my first chapter, you will see my journey laid out exactly like this. You will also see in chapter two what happens next, at around the midpoint of whatever faith stage model you use: you begin to have doubts and questions about everything, and everything you counted on to keep you strong, confident and growing in your faith suddenly no longer seems to work. This happens precisely and ironically in the midst of when you think you are finally strong and "mature" in your faith, feeling on some level like you have "arrived" and are having a positive impact on people's lives. What follows is a period of darkness, struggle, withdrawal and inward searching, followed by the emergence of some version of faith that is different from before: chastened, less theologically rigid, more generous and comfortable with ambiguity, and increasingly seeing faith as being primarily about realizing union with the divine and all creation.

By the time of this first retreat, I had already begun reading James Fowler's book *Stages of Faith*, and it didn't take me long to locate myself within the stages of faith framework. Moreover, I found that the classic writers of the spiritual life had been documenting this type of faith journey for centuries, and that was comforting knowing this path was normative for faith, not due to some big failure on my part. And, at least one implication: perhaps it was actually *God* leading me through this – it wasn't an accident or a misstep on my part – but maybe it was intentional and had some grand divine purpose, and somewhere down the road would be a better place.

So, when at that first Pilgrim's Process retreat Craig revealed the stages of faith as the framework of his spiritual formation process, it was deeply comforting to me, and confirmed to me that this was the right thing for me to be involved in, despite some of the language and ideas being a bit more evangelical than I considered ideal.

At each retreat, Craig gave us a book or two, and at this first retreat, he gave us *The Critical Journey: Stages in the Life of Faith* by Janet O. Hagberg and Robert A. Guelich. This book and Craig's teaching basically used a stages framework similar to Fowler's, but of particular resonance with me was the added emphasis on *The Wall.* The Wall is not usually spoken of as a faith stage in and of itself, but as part of the midpoint struggle and inward journey. The image of The Wall – an actual barrier that impedes your ability to get on the other side of it – is ultimately better than any explanation of it. That's partly because it's different for each person. For some, The Wall is not that formidable, and it is relatively quick and easy to get through, even to the point of them not perceiving it being a real barrier. But for others – including me – it is a long and excruciating process, and the most critical part of the whole journey.

People who go through The Wall are changed by it. Some lose their faith, and those who keep their faith have a different faith than they had at the earlier stages, with a revised view and image of the divine. While all don't end up in the same place theologically on the other side of The Wall, it is safe to say that all come out humbled, with God less likely to be in a box, more comfortable with mystery, and less doctrinally dogmatic.

Generally speaking, The Wall is about *letting go*. Precisely *what* needs to be let go of? That differs from person to person, and is perhaps even a bit ambiguous. Even years later, I don't know that I have a complete hold of all that was going on inside me during that time. But, for me, I think a lot of it had to do with *certainty*. While I think that different people have varying levels of need for certainty, with some needing more and some needing less, I think *all* people want to be certain of some key things; otherwise, we can feel unmoored in our lives. Before The Wall, I had a pretty big need for certainty, a real *need-to-know*, especially regarding God and theology. The Wall largely broke me of that. The tearing away of my need for certainty at times felt like having my fingernails ripped out with pliers.

A key part of my Wall experience really struck me during and immediately after that first retreat: my assumption and pride that I was generally right and knew best considering all things spiritual and theological. This was especially true as it concerned the church. Since I moved past the *learning-and-belonging* stage of my faith, and into the *ministry* stage (which largely coincided with our move to Kansas City in the early '90s), there was a similar pattern to my church involvement, which went something like this: When we first began attending a church, I would be all bought-in and enthusiastic about it. But over time, I would see problems, generally with church direction and leadership. Sometimes I had my own thoughts about what was ailing the church and how to fix it. But, often it was the result of me reading a book that – again – I would get very enthusiastic about, and compare the ideas of that book with the reality of the church, and feel like this new idea I had encountered was *the* answer to eradicate the gap between current reality and the ideal to which God was calling us. This, of course, was exemplified by my pursuit of an alternative church service at RidgePoint or a RidgePoint church plant after reading *The Emerging Church* in 2004.

The realization of this spiritual pride hit me hard as I was driving home from the first retreat. It dawned on me that I really had no idea how to fix the church, and it had been sheer folly for me to think otherwise. I began weeping so hard that I almost had to pull my car over. When I arrived home, I told Michelle all that happened on the retreat, and I again wept as she held me. I experienced extreme grief over not just my recently realized spiritual pride, but also over all the losses (real, imagined, and potential) of my faith transition – loss of certainty, my previous conservative evangelical faith package, the conservative evangelical community at large and in particular at RidgePoint, and changed and/or potentially broken personal relationships. It all fell hard upon me, and the anxiety of all I had been wrestling with over the past couple of years collapsed into profound, utter grief.

This grief remained days after the retreat, and threatened to take over my life. I had clear signs of depression, exacerbated by difficulties sleeping. So, I made a trip to my doctor in late January and was put on Xanax and Trazadone (an old-school antidepressant that doubles as a sleep aid), of which I still take nightly small doses to this day.

*Supplemented with a Healthy Dose of Beer and Rock 'n Roll*

Around this same time, I initiated a weekly meeting of a group of guys that became known as Mug Club. As you might guess, the name came from the Mug Club at Barley's Brewhaus that my friend Jim had introduced me to earlier that month. I reached out to five guys who had been part of the now defunct Life Group to see if they would be interested in meeting once or perhaps even regularly to have a beer or two and discuss various topics like theology, spirituality, and whatever else came up. We met for the first time at Barley's in late January as a test-drive of what a beer-and-theology-centered meeting might look like. We all joined Barley's Mug Club that same day and decided we wanted to do this weekly. I met with these particular guys weekly for over two years, and some version of this group met regularly for several years after that. Even now, a few of us meet periodically as we can and still call it Mug Club, even though Barley's Mug Club no longer exists and we usually don't meet at Barley's. (When Barley's dissolved their Mug Club, they let all members take their own personal, special mug home, and mine sits proudly on a shelf in my office to this day.)

This weekly time with these guys was very important to me, especially in 2007 and 2008. I could come completely as I was: depressed, confused, anxious, or whatever. Most of the other guys were going through some version of a life and/or faith transition as well, so it served as a safe outlet for all of us. It didn't fix all of our problems –

certainly not mine – but it made things seem at least a bit more okay because I wasn't alone in it. I will be forever grateful for that group and the comradery we had.

Also in January, my friend Randy, who had been on-staff with me at RidgePoint for a while as youth minister, and who is quite a guitarist, had the idea of starting a blues/rock band. He recruited several others from RidgePoint, including my friend Dave who plays a mean harmonica, and me on bass. We began practicing, and eventually began playing gigs later that year. While not overtly related to my spiritual journey, the band became a much-needed fun distraction from my tumultuous theology wrangling, and a version of this band still featuring Randy, Dave, and me is still alive and rockin' to this day.

*Alternative Service Redux*

An eventful and turbulent January finally passed, and on February 9th I got this email from Brandon, a friend from RidgePoint:

> *Do you have a copy of the "alternative service" dissertation you gave to the elders? May I have a copy? Thanks.*

I answered back later that same day:

> *Dissertation attached. Its focus on age (i.e., 18-34-year olds) became a bit of a distraction to me and the recipients (the elders), and shortly thereafter I regretted the emphasis on age rather than on mindset (i.e., postmodern). But do with this whatever you desire.*

While I was curious about why Brandon wanted my *Emerging Generations* proposal from over two years earlier, I was too mired in my own theological and emotional turmoil to give it much thought or attention.

A couple of weeks later, I found out. I wrote this in my journal on Monday February 26, 2007:

> Yesterday was a very interesting day. I did not go to RidgePoint yesterday morning. I did, however, go to Jacob's Well at 5:30, and I asked Dave (my friend the harmonica player) to go with me. He's been part of the What's Next team at RidgePoint who made

recommendations to the elders a week ago Thursday, and then got feedback from them just this past Thursday. One of their recommendations: an alternative service that is more "emerging" in nature on Saturday night. Unbelievably, they got approval to do it for the summer. So, when I called him to see if he wanted to go, he very quickly said yes. We had good conversation. Of course, many are already asking the question – and it will likely increase as more people find out about it – of what my role will be in it – given my proposal to do something similar from 2004 (which, of course, is very ironic). I told Dave that the issues for me now are primarily theological, which very well may prevent me from becoming part of it. It will be interesting to see how it progresses. God, guide their efforts, and guide me regarding what I should do.

So, mystery solved on why Brandon wanted my alternative service "dissertation." He was also on the What's Next team (which I knew existed, but in my effort to distance myself from the church, purposely knew very little about), and he and Dave had been tasked with being the point persons to plan and lead this newly approved Saturday night alternative service.

On that same Monday, RidgePoint's potential upcoming alternative service was a main topic of conversation at Mug Club. From my journal the next day:

> Once again, a very interesting day yesterday. We had Mug Club, and we did indeed get into the RidgePoint alternative service, and I got strong encouragement from the guys to at least strongly consider pursuing involvement in it. Every excuse I came up with they had an answer for – including the issue of my theological unsettledness. One was especially vocal and persuasive. His point: I'm NEVER going to "arrive" at a place where I'm completely settled, and I need to get comfortable with that, and it should be OK to work all of that out within the context of leadership – much the way Rob Bell has/is, and Brian McLaren (and Dan Poole from A New Kind of Christian). That admittedly has some resonance. In some ways, I want nothing more – it's what I dreamed of for several years. In other ways, I'm terrified, especially of getting involved in something with folks that may not be likeminded and having to feel like I have to pretend to think about things a certain way, or get embroiled in a "heresy trial"

of some sorts. Right now, I'm just simply not going to let myself get into something like that. The possible solution: I don't ever get positioned as the leader, but rather am part of a leadership team. I am very upfront with them, to make sure they know where I am on things, and if they're okay with it, then great. I also would absolutely not want to be the one who is the primary liaison/interface with staff or elders.

Will this thing be the answer to my prayers the past few years? Will this be what allows my family and me to stay at RidgePoint? Or, will it fail miserably and/or be the straw that breaks the camel's back, leaving me feeling even worse and more dislocated? I don't know. But God, I do want your will. I like having the sense of excitement about something church-related again.

A few days later, an announcement went out to all RidgePoint leadership about the Saturday night alternative service, and I began getting questions about my involvement. I also began serious conversations with Dave and Brandon about what my role and involvement might be. I was cautiously excited and optimistic, but also reticent and nervous. Michelle too was hopeful for me and supportive, if somewhat unsure. On one hand, it seemed too good to be true, given my desire for and efforts towards something like this the past couple of years. On the other hand, the timing couldn't be worse, given my low emotional and spiritual state. I was very reluctant to take a visible, public role again at RidgePoint so soon after relinquishing my visible, public role – it had only been two months earlier! But, I ultimately felt that, at a bare minimum, I had to explore it; it was an opportunity that was just too serendipitous to pass up.

So, in the matter of a couple of weeks, I went from actively distancing myself from RidgePoint and being consumed by my theological struggles, to being in the thick of discussions to be part of a leadership team for an alternative service at the very church I was trying to distance myself from... and a service that sounded very similar to what I had proposed creating and leading the previous two years. Sounds crazy, doesn't it? Maybe just crazy enough to work.

*Spring Flowers*

Throughout the spring, I continued to grapple with what my role in the new Saturday night RidgePoint alternative service would be. Michelle was increasingly on-board and excited about it. Our good friends Dan and Lana joined in, as did our friends Phil and Terri, with Terri joining Dave and Brandon as part of the leadership team. Phil and Terri had become friends with Zach, a leader in a local youth ministry organization who was unsettled church-wise and in search of some sort of emerging church alternative (he had attended Jacob's Well for a while, but found the commute daunting from his suburban home). So, in early March a lunch was scheduled for Brandon, Dave and Terri to meet with Zach and discuss if RidgePoint's alternative service would be something he would be interested in not only being part of, but potentially help lead (which he did). And of course, I was invited to attend, and of course, after agonizing over it for a few days, I ultimately did, starting me on the slippery slope toward full involvement and leadership.

But as my leadership role ramped up throughout the spring, I continued to feel very vulnerable as I eased my way back into a leadership position. In particular, I feared being "found out" theologically. I was scared that once those involved in leadership of the alternative service – and certainly the elders at RidgePoint who were overseeing the development and launch of the service – found out how much I was not only questioning, but moving beyond, traditional evangelical orthodoxy, I would be rejected and cast out as a heretic. My emotional and spiritual state was not ready for that kind of rebuff; I feared it would push me over the edge. I tried here and there to bring up my theological differences, but they were either not fully perceived or understood (and I was not very adept at articulating them at that point), or received generously. So, what I feared never completely happened, but I continued to be on edge theologically around other people – even those closest to me – for several years to come.

Of particular concern was my evolving view of Jesus's death. Since I entered conservative evangelical Christianity in my late teens, I had been taught and had fully accepted that Jesus's death had one singular meaning, and that meaning was not only central to the gospel, it was actually THE gospel. That meaning is often called *penal substitutionary atonement*, and is essentially this: We as humans are all sinners, and while God loves us, he hates sin. Sin is abhorrent to God, an offense and a crime against his holiness, and deserves punishment, that some sort of penalty be paid for it. We sinful humans are unable to do anything to pay this penalty, and because God can't stand sin, and justice must be served, our sins result in our separation from God, and ultimately in death and being sent to hell. But, God in his grace and mercy sent Jesus, the sinless Son of God, to die on a cross as a sacrifice for our sins, paying the penalty our sins deserved, fully absorbing God's punishment for our sins as our substitute, saving us from hell and making it possible for us to be with God now and for eternity in heaven.

For conservative evangelicals, questioning this view of the atonement was tantamount to questioning Christianity as a whole. But I had begun having some misgivings about this view of Jesus's death about a year earlier, and this issue more than any other had confounded me and driven my theological angst over the previous six months.

There are entire books devoted to atonement theories and pointing out flaws in the logic of penal substitution, so I'll never do it justice here. But, ultimately, it comes down to this: what does it say about God that he needs a payment, a violent blood sacrifice, in order to forgive us our sins and be in communion with us? Even we sinful humans, at our best, can find it in our hearts to love, accept and forgive those who sin against us without a demand for punishment, payment or violence. If we, the sinners that we are, can do this, then why can't God? A typical answer is that God is holy and perfect, we aren't. But what does it actually mean to be holy and perfect? Does it mean holding impossibly high standards for all sorts of behavior, but being *less* loving, accepting and forgiving than we are? Seriously? Is God less loving than us? Does it mean being unmoved by repentance and brokenness unless it is accompanied by a substitutionary violent payment of blood? Is God really that vengeful and violent? Certainly parts of the Old Testament (and even some in the New Testament) would point to that, but how do we square a God who demands violence, punishment and blood sacrifice with a God of grace and love? Why in many places in the Bible does God seem to be able to forgive and accept people *without* payment or punishment? Jesus accepted and forgave countless people without it, as did the allegedly wrathful and vengeful (and certainly seemingly schizophrenic) God of the Old Testament in many places.

I had no ultimate answers for these questions in the spring of 2007. I did not know what to believe about Jesus's death, I just knew I no longer believed in penal substitutionary atonement, and I knew that would be a serious threat, and likely my death knell, to the leaders of RidgePoint, and quite possibly to those involved in the alternative service leadership as well. So, I mostly kept it on the down-low. As time progressed, I began to discover attractive alternatives to penal substitutionary atonement, and I tried to subtly work those into any of my voicings of Jesus's death, but it would be over a year before I fully confessed my jettisoning of penal substitutionary atonement to even my closest friends.

But, all in all, my increasing involvement in planning the launch of the Saturday night service served to lessen my theological angst a bit. And, outside of the alternative service leadership team, I otherwise continued to maintain my distance from RidgePoint, especially staff, elders and leadership. But, an emerging problem could not be ignored: my family members were beginning to express increasing concern about their experience and interactions at RidgePoint.

One Sunday night my daughter Erin came home from youth group crying after being confronted by a leader about her lack of recent attendance. But her distress was bigger than youth group. The way she put it would prefigure her ability to be brilliantly articulate as an adult: *I do not like church, and I really don't like it that I don't like church.* To which I could authentically say a hearty "Amen!" Jordan and Haley had both complained about RidgePoint recently too, saying that they just didn't like it much anymore. Michelle had been involved in RidgePoint children's ministry leadership for years, but more and more was torn between that and being heavily involved in our kids' schools. She was getting the message from RidgePoint leaders – implicitly for sure, and at times explicitly – that children's ministry was the *right* choice, the one aligned with God's will, and opting for increased involvement in our kids' public schools would be choosing "lesser things." Increasingly this did not sit well with Michelle – is life really that neatly divided between church/"spiritual" things, and family and everything else? – which caused her discontent to grow.

Being unsettled personally was one thing, but now I felt like it had spread to some degree to my entire family. And, this upped the ante considerably regarding the alternative service. Not only did I view it as my last chance to find a spiritual environment that worked for me within the RidgePoint ecosystem, I now viewed it as a last chance for my family as a whole.

In the meantime, though, I had a couple of mystical experiences in the spring of 2007 that were harbingers of where my faith would go in the coming years. Ironically, the first of these was during a RidgePoint service. From my March 2007 journal:

> I had a mystical experience yesterday during the communion time at RidgePoint. I was onstage with the band listening to just the piano play. It was a beautiful song, and I just closed my eyes and listened and let it wash over me. Soon I was imagining Jesus pouring water over me and then gently rubbing balm on my wounds, and then ultimately looking me in the face and gently wiping away my tears. I think this was real, and it moved me profoundly and deeply. I wanted to bottle it so that I could experience that any time I wanted.

Another experience was during the second Pilgrim's Process retreat at Conception Abbey in April, and later I would look at it as a significant turning point in my journey. From my April 2007 journal:

> The most meaningful thing that happened to me over the weekend: I was walking Saturday afternoon through their apple orchard. The trees were just beginning to bud. I looked closely, and noticed that they had been pruned. One of Craig's favorite metaphors for the Wall is pruning, from John 15. It hit me like a ton of bricks (and I believe this was God telling me this): this apple tree is a metaphor for me. After significant pruning and a long winter with no fruit, I am beginning to show signs of new life. I don't have full blown fruit yet (for the apple trees, that will take until September), but I feel that I'm slowly springing back to life. At least for that brief moment, it made me extremely grateful for the Wall. Thank you for that moment, Lord, and for the whole weekend. Although I'm sure there will be setbacks and letdowns (I had a bit of one yesterday), let the apple tree generally be true of me.

It is true that "setbacks and letdowns" continued, and I was in no way through the Wall. But, I still mark that moment as the time when things turned, when I began "slowing springing back to life," when it all started getting progressively better instead of just getting worse. And, involvement in planning for the debut of the upcoming Saturday night alternative service increasingly occupied my time and attention, leaving less time for distressing theological ruminations.

*It's Show Time!*

As June 2nd – the opening service of the now named *The Gathering at RidgePoint* – approached, it became more and more clear that I would have a prominent leadership role. Of course, one of the things we had to decide was what we were actually going to talk about in not only our first service, but in weeks and months following that. We developed some core values for the Gathering and decided to do an overview of those values in the first service, and then in the weeks that followed, we would take each value one at a time, devote a service to it and talk about it in more detail.

Another big decision: who would deliver the message/sermon during the opening service? This was discussed throughout the spring, and I think the main candidates were Brandon and Zach. Brandon was very smart and articulate, and had delivered several well-received messages at RidgePoint over the previous couple of years. And Zach was a preacher for a living. Dan had certainly preached at RidgePoint many times over the years, but he didn't seem to have much interest in being the lead-off batter.

When those discussions began, I didn't consider myself a candidate at all. After all, from the beginning discussions about the Saturday night service in late February and early March, I said I didn't want a visible leadership position given my unstable theological and emotional state. So, I took myself completely out of the running for delivering the opening message. However, as April turned to May, and as my leadership role increased beyond what I initially imagined, Brandon and Zach began having reservations about doing it themselves. With Zach, it was mostly that he was new to us and to RidgePoint, and he felt it was not entirely appropriate to have him do it given his and RidgePoint's lack of mutually familiarity. With Brandon, his budding reluctance was a bit more mysterious… but he was a mysterious guy. I never did know why he opted out, he just eventually insisted that it not be him, giving some spiritualized version of "I'm just not feeling it" as his reason. (I now suspect that by this point he was not feeling entirely comfortable with the direction of the Gathering; a few months later, he and his family would leave the Gathering and RidgePoint as a whole.)

So, guess what? (You could see this coming a mile away, couldn't you?) I conceded to deliver the opening message, using the story of Jesus's encounter with Zacchaeus from Luke 19 (yes, the "wee little man" from that insufferable children's song) as the text that revealed *all* the various values of the Gathering at RidgePoint. (And, yes, it was definitely a stretch in certain places, but I carried on the well-worn traditional of being able to make the Bible say just about anything I damn well please, thank you very much.) Further, I gave the message at three of the first six Gathering services, making me the most visible leader of the Gathering in its first couple of months.

If you had told me in March that I would be taking that kind of visible church leadership role again, that soon after crashing in January, I would have told you there was absolutely no way.

Way.

Richard Rohr, a Franciscan priest that has been very influential in my post-deconstruction spirituality and theology, says: *We do not think ourselves into new ways of living, we live ourselves into new ways of thinking.* This is what largely happened to me during the spring and summer of 2007. As I immersed myself into this small community of people leading and attending the Gathering, doing life together, and as I increasingly took on a leadership role and worked through some of my theological grappling publicly via some of my Gathering messages, my theological unsteadiness became less acute and had less utter dominance over my life. I still had *a lot* of thinking and wrestling left to do (I mean, that's me, that's what I do), but the living of it within this community, most of whom were also on some version of this journey, served to coalesce some of my theological thinking and stabilize me a bit.

The last of those three messages that summer got me in some trouble. (It was delivered on July 7, 2007 – 7.7.7 – which I think biblically is the perfect number. I have no idea what that means for this story, but nevertheless I felt obliged to point it out.) The Gathering value for the day was *Inclusive*. I said many controversial things in my *Inclusive* message. I suggested that the Bible wasn't as clear on everything as we might have been led to believe. I said that our interpretation of Scripture was at least partially a result of our cultural context, and I explicitly pointed out what the cultural context was: white suburban conservative Christianity. I said that there were good sincere people in different cultural contexts with beliefs very different from ours, and we cannot just write them off as misguided or evil because of that. I talked about valuing orthopraxy (right practice or action) above orthodoxy (right thinking or belief). I was also by far the most open I had been publicly up to that point about my tumultuous spiritual journey the previous three years; I essentially used it to "come out" spiritually, giving a very abridged version of what you've read about my journey so far.

While this message definitely elicited some positive responses, it also caused alarm for some, and probably caused a few people to quit coming to the Gathering. A couple of months later at a Gathering leadership meeting with the elders, some expressed concern about the Gathering's theology, particularly mine, and cited some of the things I said in my *Inclusive* message as cause for concern. So, my suspicions that RidgePoint leaders would be taken aback if they really knew how my theology was evolving were validated. But in the midst of this, I continued to receive encouragement and acceptance from one of the elders, and from the Gathering leadership, who were quickly becoming my best friends in the world.

Regardless, I came away from the first six weeks of the Gathering, where I delivered three of the messages and planned pretty much all the rest of the content including music, very depleted and burned out. After stepping away from a public role for five months, being thrust back into the spotlight, despite being exhilarating in many ways, was perhaps too much too fast. So, I dialed back my involvement for about a month, only to ramp up again as we went into the fall.

*The F-word (Fall; what did you think I meant?)*

As summer turned to fall, I had a lot on my plate. I had a busy job and three teenagers with full schedules, including a high school senior (Erin). The Gathering continued to consume most of my extra time and attention. After a robust beginning (over 100 in attendance at the inaugural service in early June), it had dwindled to a few dozen by fall. We felt we were being hurt by the Saturday night time slot, so we petitioned the elders to move the service to Sunday morning at a facility across the street from RidgePoint, which we got approval for and began in November. It didn't dramatically change our attendance, but just meeting offsite from RidgePoint in a different space (we had been meeting in the main auditorium, same as the main Sunday services) helped us feel more autonomous and allowed us to more rapidly evolve into our own thing. After our first Sunday morning gathering, I wrote in my journal that "it felt like something new was being birthed." Indeed it was.

That fall I continued to feel increased freedom to express new theological leanings within the context of the Gathering. My emerging theology was decidedly optimistic. God was no longer a judge and torturer, but a transformative presence desiring to make his generous and inclusive kingdom more and more manifest in this world, and we were partners in making that happen. I was increasingly propagating this version of the gospel. But, sometimes real life crashed headfirst into this idealism. Recent conflicts at RidgePoint, especially with some of the elders, as well as a recent incident or two with my children, had made me ripe for a good gobsmacking. The demise of some friends' marriage that fall did just that.

The husband was part of my Mug Club group, and the couple had been part of our previous New Kind of Christian Life Group. In September, the wife expressed unhappiness and separated from the husband. He was reeling, and I spent hours and hours talking with him in person and on the phone that September and October. One of the other Mug Club guys was convinced she was having an affair, and some of the other guys thought that too. The husband initially resisted that notion, and I did too, not because I didn't think it was possible, but because I didn't see clear cut evidence for it yet, and I wanted to believe the best about the wife. Well... the husband and I were proven wrong, as he ultimately found evidence of a relationship with another man on the wife's phone and confronted her, and she confessed.

This was pretty jarring to me. Shortly after hearing of the wife's affair, I wrote this in my journal in October 2007:

> Am I just hopelessly naïve? Is that what this stage of my life is all about – showing me how fucking horrible and broken and hurtful people can be, that believing the best and having hope are for naïve idealists? It hurts. Where does the kingdom of God, bringing heaven to earth, his will being done on earth as it is in heaven – what I taught about this past Saturday night – come in here? Is it a pipe dream? Will I hold on to the hope of its reality in spite of evidence to the contrary? Lord, I don't want to lose hope. I want to hold onto hope, hold onto you being able to transform lives and this world, but sometimes everything I see shouts loudly to the contrary. But I also do not want to be naïve. Help me, Lord. I admit to being pretty humbled by all of this.

The use here of the f-word profanity was a first in my journaling. After developing a fairly adept cussing habit in high school, I had sworn (no pun intended) off cursing shortly after converting to conservative Christianity in my late teens. It was one of the many no-no's of '80s' evangelicalism – no hells, no shits, and certainly no fucks or goddamns. Once I broke the habit, I mostly continued to be an avid non-swearer well into my 40s (I suppose I occasionally slipped in a hell or damn here and there, but that was it, and those were few and far between). But like my theology and worldview, my language would evolve as I proceeded through my journey. You can judge for yourself whether that's good or bad (I'm sure some of you will see it as decidedly bad), but it certainly is reflective of the liberty I increasingly felt (and continue to feel) breaking free from the shackles of conservative Christianity. And while I'm tempted to add more and more swearing as I write further, reflecting that aspect of my journey, I realize that some of you could be offended and distracted by that, and so I will do my best to keep it to minimum. But, I do subscribe to the notion that nothing packs a verbal punch more than a well-placed curse word – an adage my friend Randy (former fellow staff member at RidgePoint, and guitarist in my band) and I have joked about over the years – so look forward to a few of those in the coming chapters!

All in all, 2007 was an eventful and pivotal year for me. Overall, I ended the year in a *much* better place than I began it. I certainly didn't have everything figured out. But Pilgrim's Process had helped me put my journey within a stages of faith framework and introduced me to an array of classical spiritual practices (contemplative prayer, silence, Examen, Lectio Divina) that were helping me experience the divine and carried decidedly less doctrinal baggage than the standard-bearer practices from my evangelical past. And being involved in an upstart spiritual community, the Gathering at RidgePoint, not only distracted me from my intense theological musings, but actually allowed me an outlet for them. All of this may have tempted me to think that my deconstruction was mostly in the past. While it would never again be as intense as in early 2007, it was by no means over. I had more theological hurdles to cross.

# 7: 2008

After beginning 2007 in severe theological crisis, the emergence of the Gathering at RidgePoint later that year provided me not only with a valuable distraction from my faith deconstruction, but an outlet to begin to express and live out some of my nascent reconstructed theology. However, while there were times in 2007 where I essentially took a break from reading and thinking about theology (and Pilgrim's Process was much more focused on spiritual practices than theology), overall I was still in serious searching mode. I continued to expose myself to new authors and information that further challenged my faith and my thinking. As 2007 turned into 2008, old feelings of spiritual dislocation resurfaced, and it discouraged me that I was years into this journey and still feeling this way. I wrote this in my journal in early 2008:

> If I'm honest, I'm still trying to find my way. I'm not in crisis like I was last year at this time, and I have at least gotten a taste of finding a new theology that I think will work for me, and a taste of serving in a somewhat fulfilling way again via the Gathering. But, this thing has now been at least 3.5 years in the making, and I'm marveling at how slowly it proceeds. Stuff I read even a year ago that I couldn't completely grasp now more fully comes alive to me, and thus the stuff I currently read that I'm not thoroughly grasping will come alive to me at some point in this journey. This is something that is going to take years. Thank

you, Father, that you are with me through it. Guide and lead me as I go. Take me to a place where I am one with you, and am no longer threatened by conservative, fundamentalist doctrine.

While the Gathering itself continued to go well, I dreaded and was triggered by just about any contact with RidgePoint leadership and theology. For example, the Gathering was using regular leavened (a bible-y word for yeast) bread for communion, and a church leader confronted me about this, saying it wasn't biblical and we should be using unleavened bread.

For fuck's sake.

(Remember, I already told you in the previous chapter that there might be a well-placed curse word or two going forward. Judge for yourself if this is indeed "well-placed." And if it makes you feel any better, just replace with *frick* in your head.)

I was nominated to be a RidgePoint elder and promptly turned it down. I was then nominated to be a deacon, which I briefly considered, but it involved two extensive interviews, including one with the elders, and I just could not put myself through it. I'm not great at hiding my thoughts and feelings, and I knew these interviews would more fully expose my theological differences from mainstream RidgePoint, threatening my leadership involvement in the Gathering and sending me on a downward spiral spiritually and emotionally.

While I did my best to distance myself from the rest of RidgePoint, early in 2008 some of the Gathering leaders were concerned there was *not enough* connection and cohesion between the Gathering and RidgePoint as a whole. This depressed me, as the only reason I could be part of the Gathering was *because* the connection to RidgePoint was very loose. I thought that any attempts to bring us closer together with RidgePoint would result in a compromise of what we were doing and a confirmation of why there was tension between us, resulting in more. I knew that any more involvement from RidgePoint leadership in the Gathering would absolutely drive me away, and that felt like an existential threat to me then given the fulfillment and freedom I was experiencing being part of the Gathering. It was becoming more and more clear that I could not exist within RidgePoint much longer. The big question was would the Gathering eventually leave as well, or was I ultimately going to have to leave the Gathering too?

In the meantime, I continued to read. I read books about the atonement in a continuing attempt to come to some understanding of Jesus's death apart from the penal substitutionary theory, which I had jettisoned over a year earlier. This, as well as other books I was reading, really led me to think a lot about the character and nature of God. A big question for me at the time was: is God violent? I was faced with a biblical legacy of a violent, retributive God – not exclusively, but way more than enough to ignore. I was coming to understand God primarily as love, and I was in the process of letting go of the Bible as infallible and exclusively literal. But I was still very much trying to pull unified singular messages from the Bible, and it turns out the topic that is the most difficult to find a unified singular message on is the nature of God himself. Is God loving and "gracious and merciful, slow to anger and abounding in steadfast love" (Exodus 34:6)? Or, is God violent and prone to outbursts of anger, who will order genocide on occasion, capriciously strike people down, and "by no means clear the guilty, visiting the iniquity of the fathers on the children and the children's children, to the third and the fourth generation" (Exodus 34:7; yes, the *very next verse*!). I would have much more wrestling to do on this subject in the months to come.

Three consequential books that I read that spring:

- *The History of God*, by Karen Armstrong. I was fascinated and riveted by this book, as it spelled out the origins and history of religion in general, and specifically the Hebrew faith and the very notion of God. I was a bit rocked by the idea that the early Hebrews were likely polytheists (there's a lot of evidence for this in the Hebrew Scriptures that has been conveniently ignored or reinterpreted by the subsequent monotheist Jewish and Christian faiths), born out of a thoroughly polytheist middle Eastern culture. I was also struck by the origin of the Hebrews' god, Yahweh, as a god of war; no wonder this God is portrayed as so violent in parts of the Hebrew Scriptures. But what really shook me is how Armstrong openly referred to so many of the biblical stories as myth. As I said previously, by this point I no longer considered the Bible to be inerrant and to be taken completely literally, and I had gotten used to the idea by now that at least the opening chapters of Genesis were largely myth, and possibly selected other stories (like Jonah and Job). However, to consider that possibly the entire Exodus story – and many others – was myth? I think I knew deep down that the Exodus account contained a whole lot of myth (the entire Nile river literally turned to blood? Seriously?), but I never allowed myself to think about it much or go there, and this book forced that issue. I didn't want all that to matter to me anymore, but it evidently still did. I would soon get much more comfortable with all this, but this book was key in introducing me to those ideas.

- *The Dark Night of the Soul: A Psychiatrist Explores the Connection Between Darkness and Spiritual Growth*, by Gerald May. This book is not the classic by St. John of the Cross, but rather May's interpretation and expansion of it, based on his work as a psychiatrist and spiritual director. It confirmed to me that I was still experiencing a "dark night of the soul," still on some level in the midst of "the Wall." I felt very understood and encouraged reading this book, and I actually read it twice that spring. May also talked much about mysticism and contemplation, which was certainly covered to some degree in the previous year's Pilgrim's Process materials and retreats, but I came away from this book determined to more fully investigate and grow that aspect of my faith, not just exclusively exploring and reading about doctrinal and intellectual facets.

- *The Last Week*, by Marcus Borg & John Dominic Crossan. Borg and Crossan were among the most well-known and prolific liberal theologians at this time. I had been aware of them for years, but had previously dismissed them as misguided at best, heretics at worst. As I proceeded through my journey, they increasingly intrigued me (and scared me a bit too), as I read interviews or excerpts of their writing on the internet. They released this book in early 2007, and it covered Jesus's last week according to the gospel of Mark. In many ways it crystalized my progressing theology, presenting a cogent and compelling view of Jesus and his life and message (the kingdom of God), including his death. This book contextualized the events of Jesus's last week in light of his life and message in a way that made sense, and that has in many ways stuck with me ever since. I have re-read this book at least a half dozen times since, usually devotionally during the week or two before Easter.

*Gathering 2.0*

As spring 2008 progressed, it was becoming clearer and clearer that things were not going to work long-term at RidgePoint – not only for me, but for the Gathering as well. The other Gathering leaders, who just a couple of months earlier were desperately seeking ways for the Gathering to become more integrated with RidgePoint, were now quickly in the process of giving up on that. The lack of enthusiasm and support for the Gathering from RidgePoint leadership and attendees was palpable. As the unfeasibility of staying part of RidgePoint began dawning on us early that spring, several of us began wondering whether the Gathering would continue at all. This severely depressed me, as it was such a source of life to me in the midst of my spiritual deconstruction. But further discussion revealed we *all* wanted it to continue, and by early April there were starting to be serious conversations about the possibility of taking the Gathering out on its own.

However, there remained some interest among some Gathering leaders for us to have *some* affiliation with RidgePoint. While I was tired of all the time and energy being spent trying to make it work within RidgePoint, I agreed to make one final attempt. But, we were at a crossroads, and staying connected in any way to RidgePoint would be contingent on receiving their support, and not just moral support. While all of us were continuing to give financially to RidgePoint – we took a weekly offering at the Gathering, and 100% of that went into the RidgePoint general fund – we were getting practically nothing back from RidgePoint financially. They were simply letting us continue to exist. That absolutely had to change going forward. We simply couldn't continue on as is.

In early May, we submitted a proposal to the elders laying out a rationale for becoming more autonomous but still maintaining connection with RidgePoint. We envisioned either building out a dedicated space for us within the RidgePoint building, or more ideally, relocating somewhere else but still maintaining affiliation with RidgePoint. But, along with this was a request for regular financial support, at least $50,000 a year, ideally more like $100,000. The main reason for the size of investment we were requesting: up to this point, we had been fully volunteer led, but we were feeling that, if we wanted to grow and thrive, we need more dedicated leadership; in other words, a paid pastor. Zach was the prime candidate for this. He was transitioning out of youth ministry, and while he was interviewing for pastor positions on the West Coast where he and his family were from, he preferred to stay in Kansas City and stay involved in the Gathering. However, his wife Kim and their children were only tangentially involved. We had been meeting now for nearly a year, and they had attended less than a half dozen times in total. We always considered this somewhat odd, given Zach's extensive involvement and leadership role, but not in any way a threat to our existence. But as we considered actually hiring Zach as our paid lead pastor, it became a bit more concerning, as we got the distinct sense that Kim did not share his preference to stay in Kansas City. Nevertheless, we pushed forward.

Our proposal to the elders was respectfully if not enthusiastically received. But the day after we presented our proposal, an email was sent to all RidgePoint leadership saying that the church was about to purchase some land on which to build a future building, and that giving was currently $2,000 per week below expenses. The Gathering leadership called an emergency meeting, and we all thought it was now crystal clear that we needed to go out on our own. We began exploring possible places to meet, starting with a local Irish pub, who seemed very open – even anxious – for us to meet there on Sunday mornings.

A week later, we got some time on the elders' meeting agenda, and informed them of our intention to take the Gathering out on its own. We feared what the reaction would be, but it went better than we could have imagined. They were very gracious, supportive and encouraging, especially pastor Brad. Truth told, I'm sure a big part of them was glad to be rid of us. We were no doubt a big pain in the ass, and a significant distraction. On the other hand, the Gathering leadership consisted of people who had been very visible leaders at RidgePoint for many years, including some significant financial contributors. So, us leaving would be a blow to the church, both its ego and finances, but would be better for all of us in the long run. So, in late May it was decided: we were going out on our own, headed into the great unknown, especially considering the uncertain nature of Zach's future.

As we embarked on this new chapter of the Gathering, I felt the need to "come clean" to the other leaders on one of my big theological issues: penal substitutionary atonement. So, in the midst of informing the elders of our plans, I sent a long email to the other Gathering leaders addressing the subject. I told them flat-out that I no longer believed that penal substitutionary atonement was literally true, that there was a literal penalty that *had* to be paid for our sins, that Jesus's death was literally that payment, and so on. I told them that penal substitutionary atonement was one of *many* metaphors for explaining, interpreting, and understanding Jesus's death, but that I thought *that* particular metaphor was especially harmful because it can easily lead to God becoming a monster. And, I told them that I wanted us to be a church where we explored metaphors *beyond* penal substitutionary atonement.

I was relieved to send that email, but nervous too. Very quickly, though, I got very positive and receptive reactions to it, making me feel safe and confident going into the future with these people, in spite of the uncertainty surrounding everything related to the Gathering 2.0, especially regarding Zach's status.

By the end of June, Zach had accepted a position with a church on the West Coast. This hit the rest of us hard at first, but soon after it was mostly a relief, as we had no idea how we were going to pay his salary. A few weeks earlier we had had a meeting of what was becoming known as the Five Families (Dan and Lana, Dave and Lynn, Phil and Terri, Zach and Kim, and Michelle and me) on our backyard deck, and the other four couples wrote down on index cards how much we thought we could commit to on an annual basis to support Zach and his family. The total was $25,000, about a quarter of what they needed. That, as well as Kim's desire to move back to the West Coast, sealed their and our fate: we would go into the future without a paid pastor (and our good friends Ron and Mary Ann, who had recently returned to Kansas City and RidgePoint after being away for a few years, and were regular Gathering attendees since its early days, would soon take Zach and Kim's place among the Five Families).

*Ekklesia*

Things moved quickly from there. By early July we had reached a deal with the Irish pub to be our weekly Sunday morning meeting location, and had decided to rename our community *Ekklesia* (we pronounce it eh – kluh – SEE' – uh). Ekklesia is a Greek word in the New Testament that is usually translated *church*, but in reality, it was a word commonly used in first century Greek culture for any assembly or gathering of people that were called together for a common purpose. We wanted this word to describe our budding faith community. That common purpose would evolve somewhat over the years, but initially we connected the name Ekklesia with "a gathering of ordinary people called together for the common purpose of learning to more fully follow Jesus as a way of life, and be a blessing to the world because of it."

In late July, pastor Brad and I made a joint announcement at RidgePoint's Sunday services that the Gathering would be transitioning to an independent church called Ekklesia in one month. There was definitely some disappointment among RidgePoint attendees that we were leaving, but certainly some relief as well among those who really didn't support the Gathering existing at all.

Three weeks later the RidgePoint elders had all the people who were leaving to be part of Ekklesia – about 40 of us including all the children – come up on stage where they prayed for and said a blessing over us, sending us out to further God's kingdom. They were again very gracious, and the whole thing was very nice. But, that said, some of their words made it sound more like they were literally sending us out vs. us leaving on our own, and could even be to interpreted that this whole thing was initiated and orchestrated by *them*, part of some master plan for RidgePoint to plant a church. Of course, that was not the case, but we felt no need to clarify that. We just wanted to get out and get Ekklesia going with as little friction as possible, and be able to stay friendly with RidgePoint, since not only did we have many friends there, but some of us were planning on still sending our teenagers to RidgePoint's youth group.

It would be polite and expected to say that it was very bittersweet leaving RidgePoint, a place my family and I had called home for 12 years. After all, that last Sunday left me feeling pretty positive overall. I had some nice mutually affirming conversations with some people, and overall, the response of RidgePoint leadership to us leaving was gracious and affirming. It was also undeniable that we had met some of our best lifelong friends at RidgePoint, most of whom were going with us to Ekklesia. But, by that time, with everything that had happened, and how triggered I personally was by just about anything to do with RidgePoint and conservative theology in general, it was high time that we leave, especially me. As I left, I did not look back over my shoulder nor in the rearview mirror, not even a glance. There were no mixed feelings about it. I wasn't especially bitter, but I was definitely ready to move on.

One week later, on Sunday August 24, 2008, Ekklesia held its first public gathering at the Irish pub, which over 40 attended. From day one, we sensed a freedom that we didn't have as part of RidgePoint. Starting something new was daunting, but also very exciting.

In some ways, Ekklesia was simply a continuation of what we were doing with the Gathering: integrating dialogue into the "message" rather than just one person speaking univocally about a topic, and incorporating new and old liturgies, readings, prayers, etc. in addition to music, which I continued to plan and lead in most gatherings. At the Gathering, we had occasionally taken Sundays off to do service projects, which we continued to do at Ekklesia as well.

But, in other ways, it was a whole new world. Without the constant threat of conservative theological watchdogs crashing the party, we could more freely explore new ways of thinking, believing and living within the Christian tradition. At the Irish pub, which was housed in a 100-year-old church building, our gatherings became even more conversational and participatory, greatly facilitated by a meeting space consisting of high-top tables which seated four-to-six each, as well as a bar that could seat over ten. We got into the habit of including an ice breaker question to lead off the message, which was first discussed in small groups at the individual tables, and then discussed as a large group prior to digging deeper into the topic of the day.

But perhaps the biggest change that would shape our future was financial. We obtained the services of a lawyer, and officially became a tax-exempt church that accepted tax-deductible donations. We had no paid staff after the whole deal with Zach fell through, and we had no intention to add any. All Ekklesia donations were fully ours to use, not to pay for the staff, building and programs of a church we no longer believed in. We had very little overhead, with our weekly expenses being $215 for rent and two pots of coffee. We decided very early on that we would commit to giving away at least 20% of our money to meet needs of people inside and outside of our community. It didn't take long to see that 20% was way under-estimating it. We were getting enough donations, and had few enough expenses, that we could comfortably give away well over half of our money to people in need, and that became a defining and very gratifying habit of Ekklesia.

The nature and composition of Ekklesia's community, philosophy and public gatherings would evolve as the years progressed (for example, from a composition standpoint, it was filled with teenagers for the first four or five years, comprising sometimes up to half the attendees in a given Sunday; a few years later, they were all gone and it was primarily empty nesters). But from the beginning, a spirit of exploration, acceptance and generosity permeated the community, and this was a huge breath of fresh air to me, and continues to be very life-giving to this day. (I won't make you wait or guess: Ekklesia is still going today, now over 11 years old, although we now meet in Dan and Lana's home rather than the Irish pub.)

*The Powers That Be*

Like the Gathering before it, Ekklesia quickly became a place for me to express my burgeoning theological thinking. A key influence on my thinking in the fall of 2008 was a book by Walter Wink, *The Powers That Be*.

Wink's take on "the powers that be" (a phrase from Romans 13 and Ephesians 6) was that they are earthly systems and institutions, but that all of these have a spirituality as well. He saw spirit – the capacity to be aware of and responsive to God – at the core of not just individuals, but every institution, every city, every nation, every corporation, every place of worship. These institutions' God-given vocation, their sole purpose, is serving the general welfare of people, and when they refuse to do so, their spirituality becomes diseased, indeed demonic. Not a demon as a separate spiritual being from outside "possessing" an organization or person, but rather their spirituality arises from within them and can become demonic in nature, and the goal is transformation of that organization or person, and thus their inherent spirituality.

Wink asserted that the biblical language about powers and demons and angels and Satan reflects an ancient worldview that is mythological. Therefore, he recast all of this in what he called an *integrated worldview*, where heaven and earth are intertwined, the physical and the spiritual are outer and inner realities of the same thing, and God is within everything. This brought up a subject that I had been avoiding for some time: the literal reality of angels, demons, and Satan. I think I intuitively knew by this time that these weren't literal beings, but rather symbolic of a greater reality. However, I had not explicitly come to that conclusion, either privately and certainly not publicly. Wink's writing on this would give me a new way to conceptualize the spirituality of the world without the ancient mythological spiritual warfare framework.

Wink also wrote much about nonviolence and the *myth of redemptive violence* that pervades our world, including many forms of Christianity. Simply stated, the myth of redemptive violence is that violence is how to solve problems and make things better, that violence ultimately accomplishes good in the end. It's ingrained in all our stories and shows up in everything from seemingly innocuous cartoons (e.g., Tom and Jerry) to extremely consequential foreign policy (i.e., how we solve conflicts with other nations). Wink applied this to the meaning of the cross. The penal substitution atonement theory is totally about redemptive violence, ordained and caused by God. Wink espoused a modified Christus Victor approach to understanding the cross, but without the literal Satan and spiritual warfare motifs that some Christus Victor theories put forward. Rather, Wink proposed that God uses nonviolent resistance and "weakness" to expose and defeat the powers, which was a new understanding of Jesus's death that resonated with me, and gave me a cogent alternative to penal substitutionary atonement that I had been seeking.

Within his framework of nonviolence and exposing the evil of the powers that be, Wink spent considerable time dealing with and interpreting Jesus's words about how to respond to evil and enemies in Matthew 5:38-43 from the Sermon on the Mount. His take on turning the other cheek, giving over your cloak, and walking the extra mile were revolutionary in my understanding of Jesus. I became more convinced that Jesus was essentially nonviolent, and if Jesus was the physical, earthly representation of what God is like, then God was essentially nonviolent too. Of course, there was a lot of evidence contrary to that in Scripture, but my new hermeneutic (a fancy word for a method or philosophy of interpreting Scripture) was that Jesus, as presented in the gospel books of Matthew, Mark, Luke and John, trumped all the images of a violent, capricious God found in other parts of Scripture. Now, that didn't solve everything – let's be honest, there are some troubling things that Jesus said and did in the gospels, it wasn't all roses and sunshine. But, it took care of a lot, and added nonviolence as a key defining characteristic of my working version of the kingdom of God.

*Stretching the Boundaries*

I tested out my new hermeneutic (I didn't lay it out explicitly, but I used it in practice) in the fall of 2008 in our first major message series at Ekklesia, the Sermon on the Mount from Matthew 5-7. I planned the series and delivered three of the messages, including the one covering the aforementioned passage on nonviolent resistance in Matthew 5:38-43. I was nervous about these messages, fearing like always that I would go too far for the rest of the people there, but I got favorable responses to all of them, *especially* the one on nonviolent resistance. However, I didn't get a positive response on *everything* I said.

A few months earlier, I had read *A Christianity Worth Believing* by Doug Pagitt, and it struck me as the best crystallization of my emerging theology. Further, it was written in a very approachable and digestible way, probably because Pagitt is a pastor rather than a theologian. I was anxious for others to read it too, so I suggested we do a book club that fall to read and discuss it. About a dozen Ekklesia attendees took me up on it, and we met regularly for six weeks that fall after the Sunday gatherings. One of the chapters was about the Bible, which gave me a chance to be more explicit about my new hermeneutic, i.e., how I now read and interpret Scripture.

Specifically, I articulated in that book club for perhaps for the first time publicly a theory about how God spoke to people in the Old Testament – or maybe more accurately, how people heard God and acted on that.

My theory was that perhaps they did not hear audibly and infallibly from God as you would assume by taking the text literally, but rather heard him much the same way we might say we hear from God today: through the circumstances of life, in that "still small voice," in the voices of others, in Scripture, etc. As such, when we hear that God told someone to commit violence, to kill and slaughter people, that need not be interpreted to mean that God literally, audibly said this. Rather, he was in relationship with these people and they were doing their imperfect best to hear and follow him in the midst of their situation and culture – a culture that was warring and violent. *God* was not intrinsically violent, but the *people* of that time were, and so they heard God through the filter of normalized violence.

Articulating that was a double edge sword. In some ways, it felt good, much like when I came clean about rejecting substitutionary atonement a few months earlier. But in other ways, it made me worried, as if saying it out loud to others marked a more definitive next step in my transition away from conservative evangelical theology and views of Scripture, which some of those attending still held on to, at least to some extent. A few were clearly taken aback and surprised by what I said. No one jumped up and called me a heretic, but I got the distinct feeling that I was exceeding the boundaries that some of them had on this topic, and it made me feel like I might be "out there" all by myself.

Another incidence in Ekklesia's early history triggered similar feelings. We had a guest speaker one Sunday that fall who was studying in Rome to be a Catholic priest, and whose dad worked with one of the Ekklesia members. He said some things that I took as perpetuating a doctrine-based view of Christianity, and drew a hard line between who was in and who was out. I wished I could just brush this off as his opinion, and one that is not invalid, and that it's okay to expose people to it because Ekklesia stands for Generous Orthodoxy and we want to learn from all streams of the Christian faith. But, I took his comments as very anti-Generous Orthodoxy – but then, I was conflicted because so was my reaction. Exacerbating the situation was that most Ekklesians in attendance seemed to really enjoy it. This sparked that familiar feeling of being really far out there theologically, all by myself.

So, while I continued to get mostly positive responses to my tendency to stretch the boundaries, I lived with the constant fear that I would go too far and push people away. I so valued this community of people and their friendships, and felt I had lost so much of that with others in my movement away from conservative evangelicalism, I just feared I would eventually believe or say something so radical that they would reject me and cast me out as a heretic. It was largely irrational and not based in reality, but it was how I felt part of the time nonetheless.

And this, of course, you may have noticed is a theme throughout my spiritual journey: even though I was often encouraged by theological conversation at Mug Club, the Gathering, and eventually Ekklesia, I was always the one out in front on things theological, which often times made me feel alone and fear rejection. I was almost without exception the first among my friends to question cherished doctrine or assumed truths of the faith, and the first to vocalize it. I was often surprised by how receptive they were to my seemingly novel way of thinking (*seemingly* novel because in truth, these questions and thoughts weren't really new, they were just not allowed within the conservative evangelical stream of the faith). But, there was enough alarm or pushback expressed by people at various times that I often held back and struggled with issues on my own for quite a while before gathering the courage to voice them to others, and when I did go public with them, I did so hesitantly. It often felt like quite a burden to bear, and like I was traveling in the wilderness alone, blazing the trail for others to follow. But, in most cases, follow they did, and many have expressed gratitude to me for it.

*The Arc of the Moral Universe Is Long, But It Bends Toward...*

One of the other topics I was thinking and reading about that fall was *justice*. Wink certainly touched on it in *The Powers That Be*, and I also read another book called *Justice in the Burbs: Being the Hands of Jesus Wherever You Live* by Will and Lisa Samson that influenced my thinking on this topic. In the past, I had always thought about God's justice as being *retributive* and something to be feared – you did something wrong, and received God's punishment, getting what you deserved. But I was now seeing God's justice as *restorative* and something to long and work for. Here's an excerpt from a Sermon on the Mount message I gave at Ekklesia that fall, expounding on Matthew 6:33 ("But seek first his kingdom and his *righteousness*, and all these things will be given to you as well.") that outlines my thinking then, and largely still, on the word and topic of *justice*:

> When you think of the word *righteousness*, what comes to mind? Righteousness as Christians have used it is primarily individual in focus concerning personal piety and holiness, and "spiritual" matters, and is well suited for a gospel that is concerned primarily with getting individuals into heaven, a dualistic gospel that prioritizes the spiritual over the physical. But the Greek word used for righteousness means *things made right*, a meaning that goes WAY beyond our individual relationship with God and our personal morality, and in fact, has a decidedly communal element. Things being made right is not just limited to between me and God, but between me and you and our community and our world.

> An alternative translation (and more consistent to how it was often used in the ancient Greek language) is *justice*. The word justice is found dozens of times in the Old Testament, and is based on everything being God's, shared fairly and equally among all God's creation, and especially as it pertains to the treatment of the poor and marginalized. So, while righteousness connotes individual, personal piety, and spiritual matters, justice is more communal and earthy and holistic, and is primarily other-focused, concerned with bringing the equity and fairness and communal – and dare I say *political* – rightness of God to earth here and now.

> Now what if we replace the word *righteousness* with *justice* in some of the places we've encountered it so far in the Sermon on the Mount?

>> Blessed are those who hunger and thirst for *justice*, for they will be filled.   *Matthew 5:6*

>> Blessed are those who are persecuted because of *justice*, for theirs is the kingdom of heaven.   *Matthew 5:10*

>> For I tell you that unless your *justice* surpasses that of the Pharisees and the teachers of the law, you will

certainly not enter the kingdom of heaven. *Matthew 5:20*

But seek first his kingdom and his *justice*, and all these things will be given to you as well. *Matthew 6:33*

If we do this, then suddenly our action on behalf of the poor, vulnerable, marginalized, and oppressed is at the very heart of what it means to be seeking and living in the kingdom of God. And doesn't this fit a bit more with what we see overall in Jesus's life, ministry, and teachings, not being primarily about individualized personal behavior and morality but about how we relate to and treat others in the world, particularly those that he called the "least of these?"

Micah 6:8 calls us to do *justice* and love *mercy* – but what's the *difference* between justice and mercy? Here's an analogy:

You are standing at the edge of raging river with swift current. You see someone in the river floating by, flailing, about to drown, crying out for help. You grab a nearby tree branch hanging out over the river, and extend your arm out to grab the person by the wrist as they are about to go under, bringing them to shore and rescuing them. Then you see another person flailing and about to drown, and you rescue them, and then another and another. What you're doing is *mercy*, and these acts of mercy are critical because they save lives.

But you are not doing *justice. Justice is when you go upstream to find out how all these people are getting in the river in the first place, to see who is throwing them in, and you seek to stop the cause of all these drownings at its source.*

I must admit that I don't personally know what to do about this – I'm a bit ashamed to admit that it's just recently come onto my radar screen. But, it is increasingly shaping how I view Jesus, Scripture, politics, and the world.

The first few years of my spiritual deconstruction were mainly about changing the way I view God, Jesus, and the Bible, and were primarily *individual* and specific for *me*. But by 2008, it started significantly impacting how I view the world at large and how we live in it in a way that promotes *communal* peace, justice, and *shalom*, a Hebrew word that is sometimes translated "peace," but is more about overall well-being at a communal level. This was consistent with my multi-year evolution from an individual-and-eternity-focused gospel to a social-and-earth-focused gospel. And this inevitably had to affect my politics.

Since I became old enough to vote, I had voted in every presidential election, and every time I had voted for the Republican. It's no secret that conservative theology and conservative politics have gone largely hand-in-hand in America the past 40 years or so. It's not overstating it to say that there was an expectation to vote Republican in evangelical circles, and you would be the target of at least suspicion if not rebuke if your fellow evangelicals found out you voted otherwise. Well, I didn't rock the boat. I faithfully voted Republican through the 2004 reelection of George W. Bush, and I never once considered doing otherwise. Although I would pay lip service to God not being partisan, not a Republican or a Democrat, I had mostly bought in to the idea that Republican = good = saving the unborn = God's will, and Democrat = bad = baby killers = not God's will.

But it wasn't 1988 or 2000 or 2004 anymore. It was 2008, and my political views had changed, and that was a direct result of the far-reaching shifts in my faith and theology, and in particular, my evolving view of biblical justice. For the first time ever, I voted Democratic that November 4th, casting my vote for Barack Obama for president. I will never forget watching the election returns that night, and feeling so proud of the United States for electing a black man for president. I along with many in our nation naïvely assumed this was at the very least a monumental step forward, and potentially signaled the end of hundreds of years of racist discrimination against blacks. Of course, I now know that was crazy; we were living in fantasyland if we thought we had arrived at a just, colorblind society. White backlash happened almost immediately and ultimately contributed substantially to the election of Donald Trump in 2016. I won't turn this book into a political screed or diatribe, but I will return to the 2016 election later, because it is an important component of where I am now in my journey.

Another result of the 2008 election was the passage of Proposition 8 in California, which was a ballot measure created by opponents of same-sex marriage. It stated that "only marriage between a man and a woman is valid or recognized in California," thereby superseding a court decision earlier the same year that ruled an earlier Proposition banning same-sex marriage unconstitutional. There were massive protests and boycotts in California after Proposition 8 passed, and it stirred up much debate and attention. A key emerging church figure at the time, Tony Jones, came out in support of full acceptance and equal treatment of LGBTQ people in both legal (i.e., marriage) and church matters. I had continued to evolve on this issue, and this case definitely pushed me further along towards Tony Jones' position.

Earlier that fall, I had also DVR-recorded a documentary that I'd heard about, *For the Bible Tells Me So*, which chronicled five Christian families who had a gay child. The film was unabashedly pro-LGBTQ, and I was now becoming more fully convinced as well. But, I was also cautious because of the traditional Christian position on homosexuality, and had witnessed some resistance to rethinking it in the Ekklesia book club, as some reacted negatively to some of what Doug Pagitt wrote regarding full acceptance of gay people in *A Christianity Worth Believing*.

That fall I was feeling increasingly conflicted about this issue, especially in light of all my reading and thinking about justice. I wrote in my journal about this issue on two separate occasions that fall (and showed some progress in my thinking between these two entries):

*October 22*

One of the thoughts that I've had that in many ways scares the hell out of me: what if sexual orientation is the new civil rights issue of our time? What if "doing justice" in the U.S. right now means taking a decided stand for the civil rights of gays? What does that mean for me? I don't know, but it scares me no matter which way I think about it. If I would get behind their cause, the persecution from conservatives, including some of my closest friends and family, would be immense. But is that simply what it means now to take up my cross?

*November 24*

I'm haunted by this thought: could this be the civil rights issue of our generation – our slavery, our women's rights, our African American rights? Thus, I generally find myself fearful NOT in being afraid of going to *too far*, but rather in not going *far enough*. My tendency on some of these things is to ride the fence, or at the very least, keep my mouth shut so as not to offend anyone. Is that what I should do here, or rather should I speak out in support of a group that is oppressed? What would Jesus do? Guide me, Lord, and guide the church.

*All In The Family*

In the meantime, at the same time Ekklesia was starting up, my oldest daughter Erin had moved to Manhattan, Kansas to attend her freshman year at Kansas State University. This was obviously a big shift not only for her, but for the family as a whole. For me personally, it added to the sense of transition in my life, along with my faith and my church situation. Erin's thinking about faith issues was taking a similar trajectory as mine, and she had difficulty finding a group in college that was not radically conservative. And, when she announced to some of her Christian friends that she was going to vote for Obama in the November election, several confronted her about making that unwise and ungodly choice. She felt very alone at times, to which I could totally relate. We had many important talks that fall about faith and politics, cementing our bond over these issues that exists to this day, and propelling both of us forward in our journeys.

Another huge event that fall was the emergence of my son Jordan's depression, which stayed pretty intense for about four months. It was stressful and heartbreaking seeing our son suffer so much. Michelle and I did our best to surround him with comfort and love, and get him counseling and medication, but we felt so helpless so much of the time.

I worried and had some guilt that maybe I was a crucial cause in Jordan's depression. Did I pass my tendency towards depression on to him? Or, did my severe faith struggles over the past few years make me so focused on myself, so tormented by my own thoughts and feelings, that I simply was not as available and supportive of a parent as I needed to be? In hindsight, I think I did the best I could given the circumstances, but it nagged at me throughout that fall. But, I was thankful that both Michelle and I had experience with depression – me personally and Michelle in dealing with mine – so that we could be more empathetic and supportive of Jordan as he went through some pretty dark days.

Ultimately, all the events and transitions in my faith and family led me to consider what it all meant, and that led me to evaluate my life in light of the earlier expectations I had of myself. I wrote this in my journal in late November 2008:

> Ultimately, much of this is about shattered illusions. I think I hoped – and even assumed – that my kids would be different than I was, that they wouldn't struggle with the same things I did and would turn out differently. That Michelle and I would raise this nice Christian family and everything would go reasonably smoothly, and that because of our intentionality in bringing them up explicitly Christian (read: conservative), they would avoid the pitfalls and temptations that we had when we were young. Well, that's probably not going to happen. Can I be okay with that? Can I accept and deal with it without it leading me into the depths of despair?

> It just feels like my 40s are the decade when all the illusions I had spent my life building and maintaining are coming crashing down: my conservative faith, my pride and assumptions as a parent and husband, financial, etc. Life is harder than I'd imagined. Things don't turn out the way you think they will, and that's especially complicated and disillusioning when it involves an understanding of faith and God that largely promises and assumes that things will generally work out great if you believe the right things and/or do the right things. What a time.

But even in the midst of it all, there was joy in my life and much to be thankful for as 2008 came to a close. Michelle and I had some great times together that fall, in spite of – or perhaps at times *because of* – all the family transition and drama, including closing out the year in Las Vegas celebrating our 25th wedding anniversary with our best friends Dan and Lana. And even though sometimes I felt "out there" and alone spiritually and theologically, I was enjoying and benefiting from being part of Ekklesia, people who were becoming the most dear and important people in my life. 2008 was another eventful and important year is my spiritual journey. It would slow down a bit, but certainly not come to a halt, as I moved into 2009 and beyond.

# 8:  2009 – 2015

By the time I entered 2009, it had been four years since my faith deconstruction had begun. I was thankfully no longer in spiritual crisis. But, my journey didn't stop, nor did the struggle. I continued throughout the next few years to have days periodically that were dark and filled with spiritual angst. However, these days became fewer and fewer as the years went by. As I became more adapted to life outside conservative evangelicalism, I was less susceptible to the waves of despair and confusion I had experienced earlier. I was more and more comfortable in this post-evangelical environment, and I could increasingly read and discover ideas that radically diverged from evangelical orthodoxy without them feeling like an existential threat. Put another way: I was moving from *deconstruction* to *reconstruction.*

This chapter discusses some the more prominent themes in my journey towards reconstruction in 2009 and the years that follow. In most cases, the arguments and positions outlined in this chapter and throughout the rest of the book reflect not only where I landed then, but also largely where I am now. In some cases, I state my positions pretty emphatically, which could lead you to believe that I've just traded one fundamentalism for another. This is always a temptation when you do an about-face on important issues that drive your view of the world. I try to walk through the world humbly and open to new learning and experience, but I am not immune to the lure of dogmatism; I wasn't when I was a conservative evangelical, and I'm not now. But, I hope I have expressed myself in a way that does not unduly offend, and that I am indeed open to revising my thinking on any or all of these issues as I proceed in my journey and continue to grow as a person.

That said, one more thing before we dive in. I need to issue warning to Christians, especially conservative ones: strap in, some of this will be a wild ride for you.

*Original Sin vs. Original Goodness*

In 2010, Ekklesia read through and discussed Brian McLaren's book *A New Kind of Christianity* (not to be confused with his earlier book that I've already mentioned, *A New Kind of Christian)*, which framed up ten questions that the church must address as it heads toward a new way of believing. McLaren posited that a certain story line had been superimposed on the Bible, and says this:

> To be a Christian – in the West at least, since the 5th or 6th century or so – has required one to believe the Bible presents one very specific story line, a story line by which we assess all of history, all of human experience, all of our own experience. Most of us know the story line implicitly, subconsciously, even if it has never been made explicit to us. We begin our quest for a new kind of Christian faith by questioning this story line.

McLaren called this story the *Six Line Narrative*, depicted below:

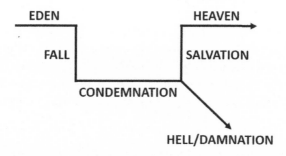

This narrative assumes that humanity starts off in a pure, pristine, unchanging, sinless perfection, aka *Eden*. But then, the first humans Adam and Eve disobey God and eat the forbidden fruit, and sin – which Augustine defined in the 5th century as "word, deed, or desire in opposition to the eternal law of God" – entered the picture. And it didn't just enter the picture for Adam and Eve. According to the doctrines of the *Fall* and *Original Sin* (articulated and popularized in the writings of Augustine), all descendants of Adam and Eve, all humanity, became infected with sin for all time. This sin causes our *Condemnation* before God, who sends us to *Hell/Damnation* as punishment for our sins. But hallelujah, God provides *Salvation* through his son Jesus to those who accept his paying the penalty for our sins through his death on the cross, which leads to us going to *Heaven* to live with God forever.

You see that *sin* – represented by *Fall* in the McLaren's depiction – is the lynchpin in the whole story, and this story was absolutely the one I bought into as a conservative evangelical. It was implicitly and explicitly taught from the pulpit, in Sunday School, in Bible Studies and home small groups, and reinforced in the songs we sung and the prayers we prayed. But is it truly Biblical? Please don't misunderstand: this story line certainly has some basis in Scripture. It wasn't produced out of thin air. There are Bible verses that could be cited to support each of the six lines. But when Scripture is read without this story line superimposed as an interpretive grid, it is anything but obvious.

2010 certainly wasn't the first time I began questioning most if not all aspects of this story. I had already questioned the meaning of Jesus's death and the literal existence of hell, and it was these issues that I believe inevitably led me to rethink the centrality of sin in the Biblical story line, and whether there were other Scriptural interpretations and theological expressions that we not as sin-focused.

Rereading the first few chapters of Genesis with fresh eyes and ears, and hearing some other voices outside evangelicalism, including Franciscan priest Richard Rohr, allowed the idea of Original *Goodness* to take hold in my theology and outlook. The story of creation in Genesis 1 describes creation as *good* seven times – the last time, on the sixth day, as *very* good.

As I looked and considered the world around me, it was undeniable that there were problems, evil, and yes, acts and attitudes that could be deemed sinful. But, I was increasingly seeing the good in the world, the beauty of creation and the inherent worth and goodness of each person... regardless of whether they claimed to be a Christian or not.

We can certainly choose to focus on the bad, but I had been taught to do that for over 25 years, and I was ready to give focusing on the good a try. As we enter 2020, with all that has happened in the world the last few years, especially in the U.S., it's more challenging focusing on the good now than it was ten, even five, years ago. But, in the midst of a world sometimes seemingly steeped in evil, if you look for good, it is definitely there.

*Here/Now vs. There/Then*

The right side of the Six Line Narrative dealt squarely with eternal destiny. By the time 2009 rolled around, I had questioned enough cherished doctrine that I had evolved into what I have sometimes referred to as *Here/Now* theology, contrasted from my previous *There/Then* theology. As I mentioned earlier, the conservative evangelical doctrine I had embraced as a young adult was decidedly focused on what happens after you die. Not that what happened here and now was unimportant, but that was at least partially because it affected what happens after you die. Even if your own personal salvation and eternal destiny wasn't in question – and mine wasn't because I was assimilated into a version of Christianity that believed "once saved, always saved" – your reward, or the size of your mansion, or the amount of treasure you stored up in heaven was absolutely dependent on what you did and how you spent your life in your time on earth.

This eternity-focused perspective definitely affected how I and other evangelicals read the Bible. Any possible passage that could be interpreted as referring to the afterlife, indeed was. A couple of examples from the end of the Sermon on the Mount in the book of Matthew:

> Enter through the narrow gate. For wide is the gate and broad is the road that leads to destruction, and many enter through it. But small is the gate and narrow the road that leads to life, and only a few find it. (Matthew 7:13-14)

> Therefore everyone who hears these words of mine and puts them into practice is like a wise man who built his house on the rock. The rain came down, the streams rose, and the winds blew

and beat against that house; yet it did not fall, because it had its
foundation on the rock. But everyone who hears these words of
mine and does not put them into practice is like a foolish man
who built his house on sand. The rain came down, the streams
rose, and the winds blew and beat against that house, and it fell
with a great crash. (Matthew 7:24-27)

I and every other evangelical I knew took for granted that these two
passages are ultimately about eternal destiny. "Leads to destruction"
and "fell with a great crash" were interpreted as ending up in hell, and
"leads to life" and "did not fall" were interpreted as having eternal life
in heaven with God. There are countless other examples of reading
eternal destiny into passages in the New Testament, and even in the Old
Testament, where it's been convincingly demonstrated that for much of
its BCE history the Hebrews had no developed view of an afterlife.

There are other places where you can read about how the idea of an
afterlife, and specifically the focus on it in Christianity, came into being.
I did plenty of this when I was reconsidering the doctrines of hell,
atonement, and eschatology (i.e., the end times). I can't do it justice
here and will not try. But, as I began to read sources outside of
traditional conservative evangelicalism, I encountered views that
challenged the assumption that Jesus was primarily about saving souls
from hell, and recast much of the Bible in light of life in the here and
now. For example, you can absolutely interpret the two Sermon on the
Mount passages above about *this* life, here and now, not about heaven
and hell later. The afterlife emphasis is the *lens* through which we've
read the Scriptures. By 2009, I was not only fully aware of that lens, but
I was actively seeking to change lenses. I became thoroughly convinced
– and remain so to this day – that *the Bible is primarily about our lives
together on earth now*, not about what happens when we die.
(Although, I certainly acknowledge that the afterlife is addressed in
places in the New Testament, just not in as many places as we've
historically been led to believe.)

So, over those four years since I began deconstruction, I went from
thinking the kingdom of God is mostly about an eternal kingdom that
starts on this earth but is primarily fulfilled in heaven and/or after
Jesus's return, to thinking that the kingdom of God "has come near"
(Mark 1:15) and "is in your midst" (Luke 17:21) – in other words, is

primarily about the here and now. I transitioned from an eternity-based gospel *about* Jesus, to the kingdom-based gospel *of* Jesus, a gospel of justice and inclusion that is good news for *this* life. The implications of this shift were revolutionary.

If eternity is no longer hanging in the balance, we can shift our attention to *this* life. And while there are many wonderful and beautiful things about this life – too many to name, really – it doesn't take long to see the tremendous gaps in justice and equality among the various people of this world. And if we no longer view the words and actions of Jesus through an eternity-focused lens, we then have to take seriously the things he said and did as he encountered those gaps. And it turns out, taking Jesus seriously in this regard is a whole hell (no pun intended) of a lot harder than looking to Jesus as primarily a ticket to heaven. It's really, really difficult to love your enemies, to welcome the stranger, to disrupt your life and help someone in your path that is hurting and in peril, to not be focused on money but to sell your possessions and give to the poor. *This* is why it's a narrow path, and honestly, one of the reasons I'm now more hesitant to identify as a Christian, i.e., as someone who is literally Christ-like. I am woefully inadequate at being like the Jesus who said and did those things. Saying a sinner's prayer and getting dunked in a tub of water, attending church and Bible studies, learning the right lingo and doctrines, quoting verses about how Jesus meets my needs and assures me eternal life – that shit's easy compared to taking Jesus seriously in *this* life.

But, I must confess that I have progressed much more slowly in my ability to see and respond to injustice and inequality than I did in my theology. In the last chapter, I wrote about my growing awareness of biblical justice. To this day I still wrestle with what it means to "do justice" in our world. I see so much inequality in the world, and it's growing. There's so much racism, sexism, classism and homophobia – and not just in attitudes and words, but more resolutely and obdurately in societal systems that persistently work to the advantage of the privileged and those at the top and the disadvantage of those on the bottom. It sometimes causes me despair and paralyzes me.

Race issues especially stymie me, particularly the historic oppression of African Americans. I don't believe anyone in the United States has suffered as much economic and emotional harm as black people. I'm writing this in August 2019, the 400th anniversary of the first Africans being abducted from their homes, shipped across the Atlantic, and sold as slaves in Jamestown. The system is still almost totally stacked against their descendants. Yes, of course, there are examples of poor and oppressed African Americans rising above their circumstances and thriving, but these exceptions prove the rule. It is the issue that I feel strongest about but have the fewest ideas on how to solve. I just know if we are going to "do justice" in America, we have to figure out a way to overcome our systemic racism, not limited to but especially concerning black Americans.

I don't know how much I had to do with this, but my daughters Erin and Haley grew up to be feminists. (Their mom is a real badass, that's probably the biggest factor.) They have really influenced me regarding the treatment of women. I have come to see that conservative evangelicalism can be harmful to women, in some cases very harmful. Every conservative evangelical church I attended disallowed women to be elders, based on literal interpretations of the Bible. Most disallowed women to teach men at all. Complementarianism, which places women under men and subservient to their wishes and "leadership," is widely taught in evangelical circles. And, the purity culture of the '90s and '00s evangelical church put a disproportionate amount of sexual responsibility, guilt and shame on females, making them shoulder much of the blame for boys' sexual desires and actions due to what clothes they wore or just by being girls. One of my biggest regrets of my past evangelical life is subjecting my daughters to that bullshit, as they both came out of it with baggage.

But, as a response, over the past few years I have intentionally read more women authors and listened to more female teachers and recording artists, trying to allow female voices to have more influence in my life. I voted for a female president in 2016 (and had planned to in 2020 too, but alas, all that are left standing at this writing are old white men). I read all the books of, and followed closely on social media, the late Rachel Held Evans, one of the most influential people in the post-evangelical world the past ten years. She was a significant influence on me and so many others, including all of Ekklesia, and her untimely death in 2019 was absolutely tragic and heartbreaking. Through it all, I've actually developed a preference for female leadership. Men have been in charge a *long* time, with their propensity for domination, control, power, war and violence. It's time to give women a chance.

Of all the areas of justice and equality, I've probably come the furthest regarding LGBTQ acceptance and rights. I wrote about my increasing conviction in this area in 2008 in the previous chapter. In 2009, I initiated the Ekklesia leaders watching and discussing the movie *For the Bible Tells Me So*, which I mentioned in the last chapter. Also in 2009, my friend Dave – harmonica player, Ekklesia leader and college professor – arranged for Ekklesia leadership to meet with one of his fellow professors who was gay, and also came from a religious background. The conversation with her was to that point the most open and honest conversation I'd had with a gay person in my life. And, although I was probably further along than most of the other Ekklesia leaders were then, being able to openly discuss and consider this topic with them made me feel like I wasn't out there on an island by myself on this issue.

The events of the next few years would push me, and Ekklesia, even further. My friend Jim, who was attending Ekklesia with his wife and two teenagers at the time, came out to Ekklesia leadership as gay in 2010. This made some uncomfortable, but we all rallied behind him, his wife and his children as they separated and divorced, and as he met and eventually married Ryan (performed by my friend and fellow Ekklesian Dan). Jim and Ryan were very involved in Ekklesia as a couple for many years prior to moving to Chicago a couple of years ago.

Tim and Julie, a couple that we knew from RidgePoint, had their son Tyler come out as gay not long after Jim did. As they divulged this to RidgePoint, they felt rejected, and some of the leaders there openly suggested that Tyler could and should reject being gay and seek to change. This caused Tim and Julie to reach out to Michelle and me, and we had them over to watch the movie *For the Bible Tells Me So*, which was a turning point for them. They began attending Ekklesia shortly thereafter and remain very involved and some of our closest friends. Tyler met Jeremy in college, and Dan eventually married them in a wedding and massive dance party attended by all of Ekklesia.

Shortly thereafter, another couple, Wally and Lisa, came to Ekklesia because they felt rejected by other churches because they were both in their second marriage. They became good friends with us and others at

Ekklesia, and eventually their daughter come out as gay. It was old hat to us by then. We had started with intellectual assent to the idea that it was not only acceptable, but equally beautiful and right to be gay. But, the experience of having dear friends that are gay, and dear friends who have a gay child, deeply solidified our conviction.

I, and Ekklesia as a whole, are unapologetically 100% open and affirming of LGBTQ people having full rights in the church and society as a whole. And now entering 2020, I will admit to having little patience with people who are not. I realize that some of you reading this may be in that group. I respect your right to hold a different opinion, but I passionately disagree with you. Some of you will point to the six or seven verses in the Bible that have been interpreted to apply to homosexuality. My response: One, not all those verses mean what you think they mean; there's additional cultural context and etymology in most cases. Two, they were written in a time when humanity just didn't understand much at all about human sexuality or biology, and so how valid are verses that speak to those issues in the 21st century? Three, if you take those verses literally, why not others, like the ones about eating shellfish or stoning people or women covering their heads? For that matter, Leviticus 20:13 says not only that same-sex relations are an abomination, but those doing it should be put to death. If you believe the first part of the verse applies today, do you also believe the *second* part, that we should literally kill gay people? I didn't think so.

Ultimately, we should let love, compassion and empathy drive us, if we believe we have a loving, compassionate and empathetic God. Shouldn't that win out over six or seven verses whose meaning and authority in the 21st century can be reasonably debated?

(For more information this issue, I suggest www.matthewvines.com, especially his video *The Gay Debate* and his book *God and the Gay Christian*, and the 2007 movie *For the Bible Tells Me So*.)

*Biblical Literalism*

Obviously, by 2009 I viewed and read the Bible through a different set of lenses than I did in my conservative evangelical days. I was finished with the Six Line Narrative lens and the There/Then lens. But by 2009-2010, and certainly in the years that followed, I had gone beyond that: I just didn't take much of the Bible literally anymore.

As I broke out of evangelical literature and influence, I encountered more *historical criticism* of the Bible. Don't let the word *criticism* fool you; historical criticism does not imply criticizing or disapproving of the Bible. But, it also doesn't just assume the Bible is the inerrant Word of God, or that it contains timeless truth. Rather, it explicitly seeks to *understand* the time in which a text was written, the origins of the text and its original historical and cultural context and meaning. Reading historical criticism in the works of Marcus Borg, John Dominic Crossan, Walter Wink, NT Wright, and others actually made the text come alive for me again, and dramatically influenced the messages I gave in the first few years of Ekklesia.

But, it also introduced me to the idea that many of the events that I had previously assumed had literally, historically happened, probably didn't. At the same time, I began paying more attention to science, biology, and archaeology, and the advances in knowledge that we have gained over the 2,000-3,000 years since the biblical texts were written. All of this made me radically reconsider many of the events recorded in the Bible and whether they could or should be considered literal recorded history – whether they really, truly, factually, historically happened.

I have already mentioned some of the passages of Scripture I reconsidered regarding their literalness. The first to go was the chapters in early Genesis. God did not make the earth in six days, literally or figuratively, and the natural universe and life on this planet certainly didn't evolve in the same literal order and timeframe. ("Let there be light" on the first day before there's a sun on the fourth day? Unless of course "light" is *metaphorical*, but that's not a *literal* interpretation, is it?) Same with Adam and Eve, and Cain and Abel, and the Nephilim (google it), and Noah and the Ark. I learned that most of these early stories had counterparts in other cultures and religions. Was there a regional flood 4,000 years ago that spawned stories like Noah and the Ark in multiple Middle Eastern cultures? There's at least some archaeological evidence that there was. But was there a literal man named Noah who literally built an Ark that held male and female of literally every species, and did literally everyone else alive in the world at the time that didn't get on that big boat literally die? Sorry folks, not a chance. I mentioned the Exodus in the last chapter. Beyond the suspect veracity of all the supernatural plagues, there's not a lot of archaeological evidence for a large Jewish population ever residing in Egypt. I wish there was, but I think we have to at least be open to the idea that the Exodus was largely myth, not historical fact.

From there, it's not like I went through a list of stories from the Bible and sorted them into "Really Happened" and "Really Didn't Happen" buckets. Rather, the lens through which I read the Bible again evolved. Now I no longer *needed* for the stories from the Bible to be literally historically true. Influenced especially by author Marcus Borg, I began to pay more attention to what the stories *mean* than whether they are historically accurate. Believe what you want about historical accuracy, but let's consider and take seriously what a story means, not only for them then, but for us now. Even if these events didn't literally happen, Genesis 1 is a stunning poem about the beauty, purpose and goodness of all creation, the Exodus is about God liberating us from those things that enslave us, and so on.

All that is general enough, and I could just leave it there and move on to the next theme. But, that feels like a cop-out. In truth, I have reconsidered the historicity of some Biblical events that put me decidedly outside of orthodoxy for not only conservative evangelicals, but for most of historic Christianity past and present.

Concerning eschatology (the part of theology concerning end times, literally "study of last things"), I no longer believe in the literal, physical second coming of Jesus Christ. There will be no actual events that will resemble a literal interpretation of apocalyptic Biblical texts, including and especially the book of Revelation. Rather, the apocalyptic texts in the Bible were used to speak in code about the oppressor. Read with a different lens, the book of Revelation is a thinly veiled swipe at the oppressive first century Roman Empire, not a literal description of how things will go down at the end of days.

Now, the idea that there is no future coming of Christ is not that novel. There is a school of eschatological thought called Preterism that interprets some or all of the traditionally interpreted end times passages of the Bible as events that have already happened, especially related to the destruction of Jerusalem and the Temple in AD 70. I agree that at least some of what is known as the Little Apocalypse (Matthew

24, Mark 13, Luke 21) applies directly to that event. But, historical criticism would say, convincingly in my opinion, that the reason the text matches so closely to the actual known historical events in Jerusalem in AD 70 is because all the gospels were authored *after* AD 70, and the words in the Little Apocalypse were retrospectively put into Jesus's mouth. In other words, the writer of the first gospel (likely Mark, which the two-source hypothesis says was written shortly after AD 70 and was a major source for both Matthew and Luke) wrote these words about a *past* event, but had them spoken by Jesus as a *future* event. (I know this seems pretty radical and controversial to some of you, but just wait, it will seem pretty tame in few paragraphs.)

Ultimately, I came to embrace *participatory eschatology*, that in living out the values of the kingdom of God – love, peace, compassion, justice, etc. – we participate with God in making God's will and kingdom a greater reality on earth here and now.

Not believing in a literal second coming is one thing, but not believing that Jesus's virgin birth is literally true is certainly another. But, I don't believe it is literally, historically true. Here's why.

Only two of the four gospels have birth narratives – Matthew and Luke – and they are simply wildly different stories. Yes, I know Christians have tried to reconcile and intertwine them for centuries, claiming the authors of Matthew and Luke were merely emphasizing different aspects of the same story. But if these two stories are read without the supposition that they are both literally true and thus have to be reconciled, they are simply, irreconcilably different. How much of either one is historically accurate? I don't know, but evidence would suggest very little of either version (for instance, there's no historical record anywhere else of the Luke 2:1 "decree that a census should be taken of the entire Roman world" – either then or any other time – and we have a lot of historical record of the Roman Empire).

Regarding the virgin birth itself: Matthew 1:22-23 quotes Isaiah 7:14 from the Septuagint, a second-to-third century BCE Greek translation of the original Hebrew Old Testament Scriptures, which mistranslates a Hebrew word meaning a young woman of childbearing age, married or unmarried – and not *specifically* a virgin – to a Greek word that *did* generally mean a virgin. The Hebrew language already had another

117

word for virgin, but the original Hebrew in Isaiah 7:14 did not use it, which makes sense given the immediate circumstantial context of that verse (King Ahaz of Judah and the impending invasion of Jerusalem). This mistranslation might have been key in the development of the virgin birth narrative (I say *might* because the author of Luke also has Mary a virgin but doesn't directly reference Isaiah 7:14, and we simply don't know if that came from interpretations of Isaiah 7:14 or not).

Moreover, the earliest gospel, Mark, likely written in the early '70s AD and undeniably a key source for Matthew and Luke (both of which were likely written 15 years or so after Mark, and in some cases use Mark's narrative verbatim), does not include any reference to Jesus's birth, let alone a virgin birth. The book of John doesn't have a birth narrative either. And, significantly, none of the other books of the New Testament, including the writings of Paul, most of which were likely written before Matthew and Luke – in some cases, *decades* before – contain any reference to Jesus's birth or Mary's virginity. So, it is possible that the idea of the virgin birth was not common when the earlier books were written, but rather developed decades after Jesus's death when various stories surrounding it eventually circulated orally, two of which were eventually written down in Matthew and Luke.

I know some of you don't like this at all. You may argue that Jesus is consistently called Son of God throughout the New Testament, and doesn't that at least strongly imply that Jesus did not have a literal human father, i.e., was conceived of the Holy Spirit and born of a virgin? Perhaps. But, there's a whole back story to the Son of God language, which was used by the Roman Empire to refer to Caesar, which is beyond my purposes here to expound upon (Marcus Borg, John Dominic Crossan, or NT Wright are good sources for that background). Ultimately, going back to the *meaning* of all this, all of these references and stories are meant to communicate the uniqueness of Jesus and his closeness with God, both in relationship and character resemblance, regardless of whether Jesus was the literal Son of God born of a virgin or not.

But, all that I've already talked about so far is mere child's play compared to questioning the historicity of Jesus's physical bodily resurrection. In fact, the vast majority of people who call themselves Christians would say it's the absolute deal breaker; you simply cannot be a Christian if you question whether the physical bodily resurrection actually, literally happened. And perhaps they're right. But question I must.

I had done enough reading and questioning by Easter 2011 that it was reflected in the message I gave that day at Ekklesia. Here's how I opened it:

> Today we gather to celebrate Resurrection... but what is Resurrection?
>
> Conservative Christians and Biblical Literalists would say that *Resurrection = Resuscitation*. Jesus was physically dead and now he's physically back alive; all vital signs were stopped, now they are back, and the evidence is the Empty Tomb. Many churches are devoting the majority of their time this morning attempting to prove this, making their case for what Resurrection means and involves. While I am sympathetic to their desire for clarity and simplicity, is it really that simple? Upon rising, Jesus didn't simply resume his old life, hanging out with the disciples, traveling from place to place teaching and healing, and so forth. Rather, the biblical accounts of the encounters with Jesus after his death are much more mysterious and mystical: he appears and reappears at will or at random, passes through walls, and many people don't seem to even recognize him. So, it seems to me that Resurrection can't simply mean merely Resuscitation.
>
> On the other side, Skeptics would say that *Resurrection = Superstition*. Nothing really happened; the story of the Jesus's Resurrection is completely made up by desperate and probably deluded disciples. I am also sympathetic to their position – I mean, scientifically, people aren't dead three days and physically come back to life. But, the skeptics seem to forget that the encounters people had with this "completely dead" Jesus totally transformed them, and they in turn changed the world. What these people experienced in encountering the risen Christ was real – mysterious, mystical, and not easily understood or explained, but real.
>
> So, this thing we celebrate today, this thing called Resurrection,

is real, but it is also mysterious, mystical, and something we can't fully figure out or wrap our arms or our minds around.

I went on to point to and discuss the story of the Road to Emmaus from Luke 24 as exhibit A in the mysterious, mystical nature of the resurrection.

I still stand by everything I said in the opening of the Easter 2011 message. I am not in circles now where my opinion on this issue is actively sought or considered important. I'm certainly not in the habit of publicly denying or affirming the physical bodily resurrection of Jesus, and I'm content to let it all remain a mystery. But in the spirit of full transparency, I must say: if a gun were being held to my head and I had to say one way or the other, I'd bet on it not being a literal, physical, bodily resurrection. Not only does it militate against science, but also the variety of biblical accounts of post-resurrection encounters with Jesus, which again often take on a much more mystical flavor than we would expect with a physical resuscitated body.

Does that violate what Paul wrote in 1 Corinthians 15:13-19, that if Christ has not been raised then our faith is useless? Perhaps. But, let's be clear about two things. One, it seems obvious to me that later in that same chapter Paul has a different type of resurrected body in mind, something more spiritual and mysterious. Two, regardless, I find that I disagree with *many* things that Paul wrote, and don't consider him to have the last word on whether my faith is valid or not, which I acknowledge is not likely a persuasive argument for those of you who believe that the words of Paul are absolutely authoritative.

If I question the literal virgin birth and physical bodily resurrection, suffice it say that I question virtually every event in the Bible that presupposes the supernatural, that God intervenes to break the laws of nature and science. Lest I be accused of being a full-blown rationalist or empiricist: I accept that there are things that happen in this world that are mysterious and unexplained by science and natural law. Furthermore, I fully subscribe to a mystical and contemplative spirituality, which total rationalists or empiricists would deny. But, at the same time, the fantastical stories of the Bible, including the virgin birth and physical bodily resurrection of Jesus, are simply *incredible*. Now, the word *incredible* can have two meanings. The way it is most commonly used in current vernacular is as a synonym for wonderful, marvelous, and spectacular. But the other meaning of *incredible* is literally *in*-credible – in other words, *not* credible, preposterous, questionable, dubious, highly unlikely. Jesus's virgin birth and physical bodily resurrection are incredible in one sense or the other. I won't advocate strongly for either meaning over the other, but I personally have to be open to latter.

I know all of this is jarring to some of you; I can feel you bristling from here. I could have just left it out of my story. But what's the point of spending the hundreds of hours I've spent writing this to pull my punches now? I want to tell the truth, because I still believe, with Jesus (allegedly...), that the truth sets us free. And while at first all of this was jarring to me too, it ultimately has indeed set me free.

So where does that leave me and the Bible? This analogy is not original to me – I know Brian McLaren has used it, as have others – but I now think of the Bible as a more of a Community Library rather than a Constitution, Encyclopedia, or Guidebook for Living. The Bible is not one book, but many. It shows the various experiences, thoughts and feelings of a community of Hebrews and Christians spanning a millennia or more. As such, we should not be surprised by the variety contained within. Are there differing opinions about a wide range of topics? Of course there are. But, by the topics and themes we see repeated over and over again – what is God like, how can we relate to this God, what does this God require of us, what is the meaning of suffering and how do we reconcile it with God's love and sovereignty, how should we live with and treat one another, especially the poor and disadvantaged, etc. – we see not only what important issues they wrestled with, but what we continue to wrestle with as well. And while we can be tempted to write off their opinions as inadequate, ignorant and uniformed by virtue of the time and place in which they were written, we can't because a lot (admittedly not all) of what they wrote still rings true to our experiences, thoughts and feelings today. They were awed at the mystery of life; are we any less so? Yes, we have considerably advanced in our knowledge in so many areas and ways, but we are still mystified by much of life and existence. So, while I can't say that I read the Bible as much as I used to, I can say that, despite my difficulties with parts of it, it still has the ability to inspire me to be a better person and live in greater awareness of the presence of the divine.

## Who or What is God?

Questioning most of the supernatural events of the Bible was not solely due to my exposure to Biblical historical criticism. One of my most important and vexing spiritual endeavors in 2009-2011 was my attempt to reconceptualize the very nature of God. This went far beyond my earlier questions about whether God is essentially loving, gracious, and compassionate vs. judging, demanding and violent. I had already resolved that by the time I got to 2009. What I had not resolved was my increasing suspicion that the God I had been taught and assumed to exist really didn't. Specifically, was God really a Supreme Being that supernaturally intervened in life on earth, and in some way controlled it?

Nick Cave opens his 1997 song "Into My Arms" with this provocative line: *I don't believe in an interventionist God.* Thoughtful people in the late 20th century and early 21st century have increasingly agreed, and by 2009, I largely did too. What exactly is an interventionist God? A powerful Supreme Being that supernaturally acts on earth among its inhabitants, that breaks into time and space to direct people, affairs, and events toward a desired outcome. It has been up for debate how extensive the sovereignty of God is, whether God's actions can be resisted and thwarted, or rather, are absolute and inexorable, and this indeed has been discussed and disputed for millennia. But, whichever side you land on, what is undisputed is that it is in the very nature of God to *act*, to *intervene* in human history. This is what it means to be God, the very definition. God is not God without the ability to act and intervene subtly or supernaturally in our world and lives. God *is* interventionist, period.

But there are tremendous problems with an interventionist God. There's the age-old problem of evil. If God is really powerful, sovereign and in control, and can intervene at will, why all the evil in the world? You might say it is because of Adam and Eve's "fall" and "original sin" that infected all humanity as a result. If you are non-Calvinist, you might say we have free will to resist God's action to influence our world for the better. But shouldn't prayer take care of at least some of this? Were Christians and Jews not fervently praying during Hitler's rise to power and the subsequent Holocaust? If God could intervene, why didn't he? Did he just not want to? Was the Holocaust part of some divine plan?

That's a horribly offensive notion, isn't it?

There's also the problem of natural disasters. I was in the midst of struggling with the image of God when a catastrophic earthquake struck Haiti in January 2010, causing me to write in my journal:

> I still don't fully know what to do with my image of God. I still am not sure what control God has over the events of life, if any. I try to not let this bother me, and be okay "not knowing," but it admittedly affects my ability to pray. I'm trying to re-conceptualize God, and it is slow going. This is brought to the forefront by large natural disasters like the earthquake that occurred in Haiti last week. So many dead and suffering. It's natural for me to pray for God to send relief, and maybe he does, perhaps in the form of people and/or strength in the midst of suffering. But the questions about why it happened and what role God plays in that are difficult ones. I'm coming to a place where I no longer believe that God is completely sovereign, or that he operates like us at all. I don't even know how to conceptualize this, much less articulate it.

There are no easy answers for natural disasters. But, I hope it's self-evident that they at least raise serious questions about the idea of a sovereign and interventionist God.

But, not believing in an interventionist God creates its own set of problems, some of which I articulated in my journal in late 2009:

> I'm really struggling with my new view of God as largely non-interventionist. I wish that took care of all the "problems" of God, but while it does take care of some, it creates others – namely, why pray? Why ask for anything? Is God simply "there," albeit at times completely hidden and imperceptible, but doing nothing? If I believe he has a "will" – a wish for us, a dream for the world, an ideal of how he wants us/it to be – how do I believe he goes about making that happen – or does he? Would history witness to any discernible change in God's will increasingly being done on earth as it is in heaven? Is it as simple (or in reality, as difficult) as getting people increasingly tuned in to his frequency, aware of his presence and reality, and

as this happens, they get more committed to doing his will? Is this the extent of it? This would be non-interventionist, that's for sure. So, in this scenario, is the only thing to pray for is that people will get more in tune with God? But, if God is non-interventionist, is praying that prayer essentially asking for God to intervene in a person's life? I don't know. It's all confusing to me. God, I'm not sure this is asking you to intervene or not, but I still pray: help me.

Progressive Christianity, the flavor of the faith that I had largely embraced by 2009, really struggles with this dilemma, which minister and author Molly Baskette well articulates:

> The relative power of God to intervene in the happenings of our world is perhaps one of the most unresolved tenets of progressive Christianity. We all want to believe in God's interested involvement in our lives. And yet we can't believe that God interferes on behalf of some (especially, as it often plays: white, abled and Christian) while permitting others to go broke, get sick, lose children and/or die themselves.

Maybe much of the problem has to do with us conceiving of God as a *person*. We tend to think of God as if he were like us, only writ large. If *we* were God, with the assumed will and power that we usually ascribe to God, *we* would have stopped the Holocaust and the Haiti earthquake. So, either God has some mysterious plan that is simply inexplicable to us, or God is just much worse than we are, having the ability to stop horrible things from happening and just not wanting or being willing to do so.

Or... perhaps God is not like us at all. Perhaps God, who we have always described as the *Supreme* Being, is not actually a separate *being* at all. Rather, perhaps God is *being itself*.

I know this sounds pretty woo-woo and incredibly abstract, but it is in this direction that I had to explore. It's much easier to consider God just a bigger, more powerful version of ourselves... until it's not. By the time I wrote the following in my journal in April 2010, I could no longer conceive of God in this way, and I was fully into the exploration of God as something other than a separate being:

My view of God has changed over time through various things I've read, and has drifted towards God not being a "being" per se, but an encompassing spirit, the source/ground of being, life, and love. This has led me to question how "personal" God is, and whether prayer does anything at all. I'm trying to get over this, and am trying to just pray more, do more centering prayer, and just put myself in situations where I can more readily see and experience God.

As usual, my exploration involved a lot of reading, in trying to conceive of and articulate God as something other than a separate being. I read Paul Tillich's classic, *The Courage to Be*, where he talks about God as the *Ground of Being*. I read *Without Buddha I Could Not Be a Christian* by Paul Knitter, who not only helped me in contemplative practice (more on that later), but talked about God as *Interbeing* and *Connecting Spirit*. I explored Process Theology and learned of God as *ongoing relationship*, the persuasive power, lure and provocation into a future of goodness and beauty. I learned from Marcus Borg, Richard Rohr and others about *panentheism*, God in all things and containing the universe while not being identical to it (not to be confused with pantheism, God = all things). And I read about and considered many other names and metaphors for the divine: *More*, *Source*, *Is-ness*, *This-ness*, the *hum* or *current* running through everything, the *glue/energy/force* that holds everything together, *Life* itself, *Love* itself, *Relationship* itself, *Mystery*, *Ultimate Reality*.

Is any of this all that different than God's response in Exodus 3:14 when Moses asked for his name? *I am who I am*, or *I will be what I will be*. Pretty abstract stuff, more like *being itself* than a concrete separate human/Zeus-like entity.

But ultimately, all words fail in the face of this vast Mystery we sometimes call God. All words about and names for the divine are merely fingers pointing to the moon, not the moon itself. And as I let go of having to definitively name and define God, I'm more likely to *experience* this mystery, which may be closer to describing what/who the divine actually is. From my journal in October 2010:

> Yesterday evening I took our dog Maddie for a walk and had one of those transcendent moments. It was beautiful out, the

trees are probably at their peak color. I got the overwhelming sensation that I was part of something bigger. The word that came to mind to name that "something bigger" was "Fall," although I know through my readings of Knitter, Tillich, and others that words are mere symbols for an ultimately unspeakable reality. I am part of some immense beauty, some deep peace, that pervades the universe and peeks through to our material world from time to time as we have eyes to see. I want to call that beauty/peace/reality/"something bigger" "God," but I must admit, I'm so used to thinking of God as a thing or a being that I sometimes find it difficult to conceive of God as... I don't even know what word or phrase to use... which may mean that I'm on to something. Knitter calls it the Connecting Spirit, but there is ultimately no language to do it justice. But I'm thankful to be part of it, and to get glimpses of it from time to time.

So, while words fail to describe what I think the divine is, I can definitively say that I am no longer a classic theist. Theism is usually described as belief in an omnipresent, omniscient, and omnipotent Supreme Being that is separate from us. If this is theism, then I can technically be considered *a*theist; at a bare minimum, I am highly agnostic towards a classically theist, interventionist God. But I still believe in a *mysterious more*, in a spiritual reality that transcends our five senses, and that can be experienced on some level in this life.

However, I find I use the word *God* less than I used to, due to its theistic baggage, opting more for alternatives like *spirit, mystery, ultimate reality,* or *the divine*. Additionally, all of this has led me to a non-gendered image of God. Even though for simplicity, and continuity with writing about my earlier evangelical faith, I have referred to God as *he* throughout this writing, I do not consider God gendered, and largely avoid personal pronouns for the divine in my speaking and writing.

After years of a primarily rational, logical approach to deconstructing and reconstructing my faith, I increasingly realized that my intellect could only take me so far, and in fact could be stumbling block for me. I was never going to completely think my way to a reconceptualization of God or a reconstructed faith. While I could never fully give up intellectual pursuits, a parallel path for me during these years was a journey into mysticism and contemplative spirituality.

*Exploring Mysticism, Meditation, and Contemplative Practices*

Early on in my deconstruction, I was introduced to a stream of Christianity that was more mystical and contemplative and less intellectual and doctrinal. But, initially I couldn't get past the theological questions buzzing around in my head. It was only in 2007 and 2008, when the fog began to lift a bit, that these mystical and contemplative practices started becoming more attractive and promising. The Pilgrim's Process program and Gerald May's book *The Dark Night of the Soul* whet my appetite, and by 2009, I was beginning to pursue more information about this stream of spirituality, and guidance in how to put it into practice.

As I'm sure you guessed, I sought a lot of different sources of information on this topic. I read some Thomas Merton, a mid-20th century monk who almost single-handedly made contemplative practice relevant again in America. I read the spiritual classic *The Cloud of Unknowing*, an anonymous work of Christian mysticism and contemplative prayer from the 14th century. I read two separate books on the topic of silence, which also contained a lot of practical information on contemplative prayer. I purchased audio of James Finley, a former spiritual directee of Thomas Merton, who gave specific instruction and advice in the practice of contemplative prayer. And, I discovered Richard Rohr, and subscribed to his daily meditation email, which I continue to receive to this day. His daily meditations and his books *Everything Belongs* and *The Naked Now* were important for jumpstarting my contemplative practice.

I also gained information and inspiration outside Christianity. I already mentioned Paul Knitter's book *Without Buddha I Could Not Be a Christian*, where he goes to Buddhism for inspiration and perspective on a topic, and then "crosses back" over into Christianity and tries to apply what he learned from Buddhism. This novel approach helped me not only in my reconceptualization of God, as mentioned earlier, but also in my contemplative practice. I also purchased audio of Jack Kornfeld, a noted American Buddhist, who helped me integrate meditation techniques into my practice.

One of the most transformative resources outside Christianity was Tara Brach's book *Radical Acceptance*, which is not fully Buddhist, but has a heavy Buddhist flavor. A couple of years after most of the original members of my 2007-founded Mug Club dispersed, one of them contacted me one day in early 2011 saying he had read this book and found it life-changing. I picked it up and read it, and similarly found it very impactful. Brach defines Radical Acceptance as *the willingness to experience ourselves and our life as it is.* While I would encounter this basic message repeatedly in other resources in the following years, my initial encounter with it via Brach's book was particularly illuminating. Some money quotes from the book:

> The way out of our cage begins with *accepting absolutely everything* about ourselves and our lives, by embracing with wakefulness and care our moment-to-moment experience. By accepting absolutely everything, what I mean is that we are aware of what is happening within our body and mind in any given moment, without trying to control or judge or pull away. I do not mean that we are putting up with harmful behavior – our own or another's. *This is an inner process of accepting our actual, present-moment experience.* It means feeling sorrow and pain without resisting. I mean feeling desire or dislike for someone without judging ourselves for the feeling or being driven to act on it. Clearly recognizing what is happening inside us, and regarding what we see with an open, kind and loving heart, is what I call Radical Acceptance.

> Rather than trying to vanquish the waves of emotion and rid ourselves of an inherently impure self, we turn around and embrace this life in all its realness – broken, messy, mysterious and vibrantly alive. By cultivating an unconditional and accepting presence, we are no longer battling against ourselves, keeping our wild and imperfect self in a cage of judgment and mistrust. Instead, we are discovering the freedom of becoming authentic and fully alive.

> We practice Radical Acceptance by pausing and then meeting whatever is happening inside us with this kind of unconditional friendliness. Instead of turning our jealous thoughts or angry feelings into the enemy, we pay attention in a way that enables

us to recognize and touch any experience with care. Nothing is wrong – whatever is happening is just "real life."

*Seeing what is true, we hold what is seen with kindness.*

Another popular word for this approach to life is *mindfulness*, which again would appear over and over in resources on meditation and contemplation in the following years. Richard Rohr's money quote on this topic, which I have written on a Post-It note affixed to my desk, is:

*It is our resistance to things as they are that causes most of our unhappiness.*

I've continued to encounter mindfulness teachings in other books I've read. Recently I read comedian Pete Holmes's book *Comedy Sex God*, in which he advocates meeting each moment and circumstance with "yes, thank you," as a way of being grateful for things exactly as they are. I've used it recently, and it helps me to better stay present in the moment and accept what comes with more openness and less resistance.

Of course, this is all referring to an overall outlook on and approach to life. But, in order to live in mindfulness and radical acceptance, virtually all teachers prescribe setting aside space and time for a meditative/ contemplative practice. So, to try to make mindfulness and radical acceptance more natural in my daily living, in early 2011 I carved out space in the closet of my basement office, and furnished it with a chair, small table and candle, where I could engage in my practice. I tried to set aside 10-20 minutes in the mornings before work. I initially used guided resources, like the aforementioned audio of James Finley and Jack Kornfeld, to assist me and get me started. Then, I began mostly practicing in silence, paying attention to my breath or repeating words or short phrases as mantras to help keep my focus. The mantra I come back to again and again is *trust*. Trusting that life as it is, in the present moment, is enough. Trusting that the divine is present and around and within me always. Using the *trust* mantra almost invariably grounds me in ways that nothing else does.

I have kept at this meditation/contemplative practice ever since. Yes, I will admit that like every other spiritual practice I've ever engaged in, I have been hit or miss with it since I started. I can be very regular for several months, and then for some reason fall off the wagon and go a few months without it. But, I always come back to it because it makes a difference in my life. When I'm regularly practicing meditation and contemplative prayer, I have more peace, grace and acceptance, both during my actual practice and in the rest of my daily living. I also am more likely to have transcendent, mystical experiences of the divine, and see goodness and beauty in life and other people, again, both during my practice and in my daily living. And because of all this, I think my meditation/contemplative practice simply makes me a happier and better person. Rue the day I stop and never start back up.

*Fatigue Sets In*

By the time I got to 2012, I had been in intense faith deconstruction and reconstruction mode for at least seven years. It was probably inevitable that I would eventually burn out and lose interest.

That is exactly what happened. It didn't happen overnight, of course. But the intensity of my spiritual interest gradually just petered out. I think I first noticed it in 2012. This is from my journal in April 2012, writing after Easter:

> Spiritually, I have been pretty undisciplined, and I largely took Lent off this year. I really did nothing special at all. Since I first read Borg and Crossan's *The Last Week* several years ago, I have usually tried to read it during Lent, often times during the week before Easter. Didn't do that this year, nor did I even think too much about Jesus's death and resurrection. I'm trying to not judge it – my temptation is to judge it as bad and feel bad about it, but I'm trying to not do that, and just accept it as "what is."

You can see that I was trying to practice Radical Acceptance / mindfulness / "yes, thank you" with my diminished spiritual interest. In the past, I had routinely beat myself up in my journals for being undisciplined or irregular at spiritual practices – including if I went a long period without journaling – or having bouts of spiritual lethargy. But my waning spiritual interest resulted in less and less journaling. And spiritual or theological reading. The insatiability of my reading appetite the previous seven years faded throughout 2012 and 2013, and pretty much grounded to a halt in 2014, as did my journaling.

This left me in a place where I started to doubt whether any of it mattered or was real. It left me a practical atheist, or at least highly agnostic. For the first time in my life, I had moments – actually days, even weeks – where I no longer believed there was anything more than this physical universe. It was cyclical, though, as I would return to spiritual practices for a season, which would heighten my awareness of the divine. And, of course, I was still actively involved in Ekklesia (but admittedly giving fewer and fewer messages). But, overall my fatigue for all things spiritual and theological was high, and my give-a-shit was low, and so I couldn't sustain regular individual spiritual practices for several years.

Looking back on this time, I think a factor in all this was that I was somewhat disillusioned about where my spiritual journey had taken me. Through deconstruction and The Wall, I had ostensibly been broken of my need for certainty and gained a tolerance, if not an appreciation, for ambiguity and mystery. But old habits die hard, and for years I continued to pursue a cogent, consistent, rational understanding of God and faith, albeit a more progressive and mystical one. But I kept running into a brick wall. I could never come up with a revised theology that was as seemingly tight and buttoned-up as my previous conservative evangelical version. I tried to view this as just the nature of life and the universe, that it doesn't come wrapped in a bow and neatly packaged. There is no unified theory of everything, and my inability to come up with one was not a personal failure. Life, existence and whatever or whoever God is, is simply a mystery. But, I think the realization of that was at least somewhat disappointing and disillusioning, and contributed to me just largely giving up on theological and spiritual pursuits.

However, I still had times where my fading interest in spiritual things concerned me. I opened 2015 with my first journal entry in about 18 months, reflecting on the previous year:

> 2014 was an interesting year from a spiritual standpoint. Interesting meaning pretty dry and non-eventful. I would say I had minimal interest in spiritual things in 2014. I know I read the fewest spiritual books that I have in years. In some ways, my interest and my quest to find an alternative spirituality and faith from the evangelicalism I was so entrenched in for 25 years kind of came to a screeching halt. I just kind of lost interest. But, I

have some concern about that.

So then, I come into 2015 hoping to renew my commitment to spiritual practices and seeking. That's kind of a spiritual way to put it. Put another way: my goal in 2015 is to give myself a real fighting chance of not becoming an official atheist. In some ways I am an atheist now, or at least a strong agnostic. I am no longer a classical theist, in that I don't believe any longer in God as cosmic director or controller, or at least I'm wildly skeptical of it. But, unlike a few years ago, where I was actively trying to find a new version of God, I've pretty much abandoned that over the past year or so, making me as close to not only an atheist, but a non-spiritual person overall as I've ever been in my entire life.

Is that okay? I guess I'm not quite ready to accept that it is. At least I want to make some effort to see if I can get it back, at least on some level. It's highly unlikely that I will ever subscribe to some of the classical orthodox Christian doctrines that I used to. But, can I again gain some confidence (not necessarily certainty) that there is *something more*? To use words that Dan used at Mug Club last night when I confessed all of this to him, *can I still see and detect magic in the world*? I want to. And, I'm going to more intentionally try to put myself in the position to see and access it.

Will it work? I don't know. But I feel I have to try. If I'm honest, slipping into non-spirituality and atheism scares me. Not for my soul, but mostly for the people in my life. How would I explain it to them? It seems it would make my departure from evangelicalism look like a cakewalk.

God, if you are real, help me. Show me yourself. Lead me in this quest. Help me be diligent and not give up.

You can see that I felt very vulnerable about my agnosticism/borderline atheism, and didn't confess it to many people. Obviously Dan. I also told my friends Dave and Randy one evening as we were drinking beer and catching up on my screened porch. And, I told my youngest daughter Haley. She'd had some bad experiences with Christian groups in college, which by the end of her four years there left her questioning whether she believed any of it anymore. She confessed this to me one evening on our deck, which led me to spontaneously confess right back to her that I too struggled with the same thing, in hopes of making her feel like she was not alone and would be totally accepted by me regardless of what she did and didn't believe. It was the start of many conversations we've had about this topic in the years since.

Did my clearly half-hearted intentionality to right the spiritual ship expressed in my early 2015 journal work? Not really. I continued my spiritual slumber for the next couple of years. But something would happen in late 2016 that would wake me the fuck up.

# 9:  2016 – 2019

I mentioned earlier that I did not want to take this book in a direction that was too political. I also said, though, that the subject could not be totally avoided either, because it was too important to my journey. If I'd finished this book when I intended to, this chapter, which is undeniably more political than any that precede it, would not even exist. But, here we are. Proceed at your own risk.

You may have guessed by now that I'm going to talk about the November 2016 election of Donald Trump. Like many other people, I was stunned by it. I was shocked because I could not fathom why anyone would think he would be a good president. I couldn't believe there were enough people in this country that thought he was a better choice than Hillary Clinton to get him elected. (He, of course, famously lost the national popular vote by over two percentage points and almost three million votes, but now is not the time or place for a tirade on the Electoral College.)

But the most unbelievable thing to me was the fact that the group who arguably put Trump in office was my former tribe, white evangelical Christians. Four out of five white evangelicals voted for Trump, the highest of any demographic group. In fact, only characteristics like self-identifying as Republican or conservative, and paradoxically, racial anxiety in rural communities that are almost completely white, rivaled it as predictors for voting for Trump. Now, I know some white evangelicals were initially reluctant supporters, the so-called "hold your nose" voters. They despised the Clintons when Bill was president in the '90s, and could just not stomach voting for Hillary. They justified their vote for Trump with the hope that he would appoint Supreme Court justices that would overturn Roe v. Wade, and through his appointments and policies generally curb the liberal trajectory on social issues important to them, like abortion and gay rights. And, Trump's appointments and policies have done just that, resulting in even more enthusiastic support among white evangelicals as his term has gone on.

I will admit to being idealistic and naïve at times, especially where it concerns the motives and behaviors of others. I have generally been optimistic about people, and my default has always been to believe the best. The 2016 election changed that, especially regarding white evangelicals. I can honestly not think of another candidate in my lifetime who is less Christian than Donald Trump. *For his entire life,* he has demonstrated in actions and words that he is simply not a good person. *At all.* Let alone Christian. And we geniuses made him the fucking president.

I certainly was no longer an evangelical by 2016. I had cut ties with the evangelical community, and no longer had many close relationships with evangelicals. But, any resentment I had toward evangelicalism had mostly evaporated by 2016. I had decidedly moved on, and while I may have disagreed with evangelicals about many things, that no longer created any significant bitterness or anxiety in me.

The election of 2016 changed that. Not only was I shocked that evangelicals lined up to support Trump, but that shock eventually turned into bitter anger. As Trump took office, the unqualified people he appointed to his cabinet, the scandals he perpetuated, the actions he took, and the words he said only intensified my anger. And most days, my despair, at what this country was rapidly becoming, cheered on and celebrated by evangelicals, the community I used to be part of.

In early 2017 I found Crooked Media and Pod Save America, which gave an articulate voice to the rage and despondency so many of us were feeling. I subscribed to the Washington Post and the New York Times to support real journalism that I hoped would keep this administration at least somewhat accountable. And, I found and gave financially to organizations that were helping people who were the targets of Trump's xenophobic rhetoric and policies, including groups aiding refugees, working to reduce gun violence, identifying hate groups, and fighting for the civil rights of *all* Americans. Additionally, Ekklesia helped a recently-arrived refugee family from Somalia get their household set up with furniture and supplies.

From the beginning of Trump's presidency, almost *every single day* there has been some word or action from him and his administration that have caused me dismay. His incendiary language and actions towards others – the media, women, LGBTQ, Muslims, and people of color to name a few – have emboldened Americans with racist, prejudiced, and sexist attitudes to speak and act out their hate. His and his administration's vast corruption has desensitized us what we would expect is normal behavior for a president. And all the *lies*, the endless fucking lies. I could go on and on about all this, but I won't – I've probably said too much already. But, suffice it to say that I viewed – and continue to view – the election of Donald Trump as a major setback not only for America, but for the world at large. And, I believe eventually, a potential death blow for American Christianity. History will not be kind to the evangelical church for supporting Donald Trump, who I believe will go down as one of the most despicable public figures in American history.

Living with continuous unresolved rage and despair, like I was throughout much of Trump's first year in office, is not a good way to live, and eventually takes its toll. 2017 was a very unhappy year for many people, including me. And as 2017 wore on and turned into 2018, I just couldn't keep it up anymore. I started listening to Pod Save America less, I radically reduced my social media consumption – especially Facebook – and just made a decision that at least for a while, I was simply going to be less informed and less provoked. Was I able to do that because of my privilege as a straight white male? Most certainly. I could opt out of the fray for a while because my privilege allowed it, because I was not as personally affected by this administration's words and actions as many less fortunate others. But, my mental and emotional health compelled me to seek out something that was less enraging and discouraging than social media and the daily news.

Michelle and all my children, now adults living out of state on their own, were going through the same anguish as I was over the election. Erin in particular sought relief in reading books and listening to podcasts that were more spiritually nourishing and uplifting. She recommended to me a particular podcast by Rob Bell (known as the *Robcast*). Of course, I had read several Rob Bell books over the years; his *Velvet Elvis* was very influential to me in 2005 in the midst of my deconstruction. But as my spiritual interest waned in 2013-2016, I kind of lost track of him. I don't remember exactly what Robcast episode Erin recommended, but I listened to it, and it spoke to me and awakened some hope deep within me. I listened to more episodes, and I could feel myself becoming less angry, less discouraged and more hopeful. And, it was birthing a nascent interest in spirituality again.

*The Liturgists Save My Soul*

More significant than Rob Bell to the gradual return of my spiritual interest and optimism was my discovery of *The Liturgists*, also recommended by Erin. The Liturgists was founded by Michael Gungor, a Grammy-nominated former Christian music artist, and Mike McHargue, an internet personality known as Science Mike (yes, he has a very science-y take on things). They met in 2013, and formed an instant bond via their mutual spiritual homelessness. Both had been conservative Christians that lost their faith, became short-lived atheists, and then returned to a more open and progressive spirituality. (Sound familiar?) They began producing a series of *liturgies*, or guided contemplative worship experiences, both via recordings and live events, intended for people who felt left out of organized religion but still had a longing for some kind of spirituality. They launched *The Liturgists Podcast* in 2014, which grew to millions of listeners within the first year.

Without a doubt, The Liturgists, and specifically Michael Gungor and (especially) Science Mike, have been the most important spiritual influences in my life post-2016. In Michael and Mike, I heard myself, in words I didn't know I had. Years before, I had pursued a re-conceptualization of God that ended up decidedly a-theistic. As I detailed in the previous chapter, I no longer believed in a theistic, interventionist God as a separate sovereign Supreme Being. However, I didn't know anyone else personally who was going as far in this direction as I was, and the voices I did find that were leaning this way tended to be fairly arcane and inaccessible. And of course, after years of spiritual searching, I just got tired, and so I kind of eventually gave up on it. But in The Liturgists, I found the voice I was searching for, that represented where I was: a non-theist who still believed in *something more* – or who at least really wanted to – and still longed to connect with this *something more*, and had exited conservative Christianity but still valued Jesus and the Christian tradition despite jettisoning most of its orthodoxy.

I was hooked on The Liturgists after listening to one podcast, and began devouring them, eventually listening to every episode from all five seasons. I also became an avid listener of the *Ask Science Mike* podcast. I heard Science Mike say something fairly early in my listening (I don't remember which podcast) that resonated deeply with me: he said he was in some ways *both a Christian and an atheist*. Hallelujah, he was describing me! I felt heard and known when listening to Michael and Mike, their experience and perspectives dovetailing closely with mine. And feeling known and heard thrusted me back into an interest in and practice of spirituality.

What I love about The Liturgists is that they are comfortable and open with all types of spirituality and beliefs. Their audience includes everyone from evangelicals to atheists, and I love that. Their spirituality is also not static, but seemingly fluctuating. Michael and Mike in 2019 are not the same spiritually as when they began the podcast in 2014 – especially Michael, who is now heavily influenced by Ram Dass, Alan Watts and Buddhism, and no longer identifies as a Christian. On any given episode, you can hear them espousing and defending Christianity (at least some form of it), and on another you can hear them expounding on other forms of spirituality, or even agnosticism and atheism. They seem to vacillate between being highly spiritual, even highly Christian (albeit progressive, non-literal Christianity), and agnosticism, even atheism. And you know what? *So do I.* And, they don't seem to be worried about it at all, which helps me not be worried about it either.

The Liturgists are big proponents of meditation and contemplative practice. They regularly release short audio meditations. They also produced a multi-episode video course on meditation, which I purchased and we at Ekklesia went through together in early 2019.

Years earlier when I was beginning my contemplative practice, I was the only one I knew doing it. By 2018, others in Ekklesia were beginning to dabble in it, and The Liturgists' meditation video series facilitated great discussion and increased contemplative practice in our group. Now I could not only share with others what types of practices were working for me, but I could learn from them as well, and we could encourage one another in our practice. That has been very instrumental in keeping me more regular and effective in my practice, which has fed my reemerging spiritual hunger.

*Number Nine, Number Nine, Number Nine...*

The Liturgists also talk quite a bit about the Enneagram, which is a personality typology featuring nine interrelated personality archetypes, usually depicted as below:

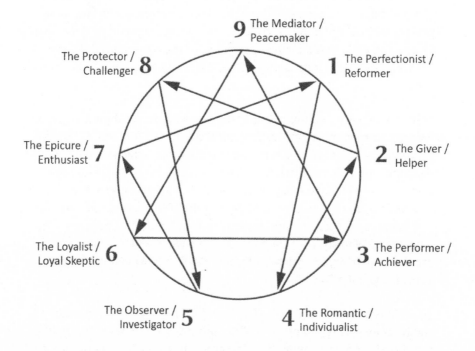

It looks kind of complicated, and in some ways, it is. But, many have found it a very valuable tool in self-awareness and transformation. I had heard about it for several years, and Erin (of course) began mentioning it more to me in early 2018. In the summer of 2018, my interest was sufficiently piqued, and I dug in deep. I listened to the two-hour Liturgists podcast on the Enneagram, read several Enneagram books (including one by Richard Rohr), and took several online tests to reveal my "type."

The typing tests are somewhat controversial. Some Enneagram teachers, including Richard Rohr, do not recommend taking a test to reveal your type. Rather, they recommend just reading the descriptions until you find one that resonates with who you are, the one that *humiliates* you the most, that makes you say "oh crap, that's me." In my case, the tests and my reading revealed the same thing: I was a Nine, with a fair dose of One thrown in (in Enneagram parlance, known as a "wing").

From my story, my One-ness is probably reasonably evident. One's are often called the Perfectionist or Reformer. Throughout my time as an evangelical, I was ceaselessly searching for a better, authentic, even perfect form of Christianity, church, and myself. I could see deficiencies all around, and I was constantly striving for *improvement*. But, while all of this is consistent with being a One, it doesn't fully get at who I am at the core.

An initial cursory reading of the Enneagram made me think I might be a Five, a common misidentification I would come to find out. I thought this because Fives are thinkers and investigators, which in many ways describes me. I do research for a living, I conduct pretty thorough research when I make a big purchase, and I tend to overthink and overanalyze things. But, as I dug deeper into Fives, I realized I am just not as cerebral, focused, and curious as they are. Or as insecure. And, when I saw who some of the famous Fives were – Albert Einstein, Stephen Hawking, Friedrich Nietzsche, Bill Gates, Mark Zuckerberg – I *knew* I was not a Five.

So what is a Nine, and why do I believe I'm one? Well, as I mentioned, the tests usually typed me as a Nine. But, for me it was more reading the description and having that "oh crap, that's me" moment, and that was especially impactful because I read it after I'd read the descriptions for every other type. In reading the other descriptions, I found something I could relate to in *every* type, especially Ones and Fives, but I also found many characteristics of the types that were decidedly not me. Until I got to the last one, type Nine.

Here are some ways Nines are often described:

- Easygoing, optimistic and unflappable.

- Accepting, supportive, reassuring, inclusive, trusting, and stable.

- Good natured, nice, pleasant, sweet, and even keeled.

- Because of many of these characteristics, sometimes called the *sweethearts of the Enneagram*.

- Good mediators and communicators, seekers of peace and harmony.

- Typically spiritual seekers who have a great yearning for connection with God, the cosmos, and other people.

All of that generally resonates with who I am, and honestly, what's not to like? So far, so good, right? Who doesn't want to be those things? If it stops there, I'd say, in the words of *Curb Your Enthusiasm's* Larry David, it's prettay... prettay... prettay... pretty good.

But, of course, it doesn't stop there. Nines also...

- Want things to be smooth and easy and without conflict.

- Tend to be complacent and willing to simplify problems and minimize and resist anything upsetting.

- Are agreeable, but they give up their own agenda to go along with others and their wishes to keep the peace.

- Retreat into their minds and fantasies, living in an imagined, idealized version of reality, causing them to be inattentive, neglectful, and remote.

- Try to escape the tensions and paradoxes of life into a more pleasant and comforting world by "numbing out" – eating, drinking, watching hours of TV, etc.

141

- Ultimately, minimize their own presence and importance, and lack a strong sense of their own identity.

Fuck.

(In other words, "oh crap, that's me" using a well-placed curse word.)

Just like I could with the positive list, I could relate to everything on the negative list as well. More than any other personality tool I'd ever encountered, I could see myself in the Enneagram – both the good and the not-so-good. I think being a Nine helps explain why my deconstruction was so painful. I want things to be easy and smooth, and I can tend to live in an idealized version of the world. I put off questions about my faith and how I viewed the world as long as I possibly could, in service of inner peace and equilibrium. But once I could no longer hold back the questions, it introduced internal – and the potential for external – conflict that I work so hard to avoid. But avoid it I could not, and this helped make my questioning and deconstruction more arduous and upending than I think it is for many people.

Additionally, as I've written this book, I've constantly fought against an internal voice saying *you and your journey are just not that important, people are not going to be interested in what you have to say*. My Nine-ness says my presence and my voice are not needed or important, and I should just fade into the background with a 1.75 of bourbon and a long list of golden-age-of-TV shows to binge on Netflix and HBO. I've persisted mostly because Michelle and a few close friends have encouraged me to do so. But, I'm still dubious that it's all of much value, because, well, I'm a Nine.

So, how has the Enneagram helped me? Well, first and foremost, it has made me more self-aware. I know that I'm not alone in trying to minimize problems and conflicts, in escapism, in going along to get along, in questioning whether my presence matters, etc. And, I can more readily see now when I'm doing these things. Having this self-awareness leads to a delicate dance between self-acceptance and self-correction (i.e., transformation). I'm in my mid-50s, and along the way I've learned more how to love and accept myself as is, full stop (i.e., Radical Acceptance). But, if I let myself go too far into the negative tendencies of my Nine personality, it is not good for my soul or relationships (it might *seem* all is okay because my Nine-ness has minimized everything that is bad). So, it's a balancing act, and sometimes I lean to one side or the other, but because of my increased self-awareness, I think I'm now maintaining a healthier equilibrium than I would without it.

In the fall of 2018, I initiated several weeks of discussion of the Enneagram at Ekklesia, including methods for each of us to identify our type. Just as happened with our meditation discussions, talking about it openly has helped all of us understand and accept ourselves and one another. It's something we can now talk about in shorthand, and can both joke about it and have serious talks about how the tendencies of our types positively and negatively affect our lives. The Enneagram has simply enriched our ability to do life together. And, it serves a similar function within our family, as Michelle and our kids and their spouses are all reasonably fluent in the language of the Enneagram.

I feel like I need to say that we are all unique individuals, and no personality typology is going to explain any of us completely. I have pieces of *all* the Enneagram types, and there are facets of who I am that are not well explained by *any* type. Humans are complex, and can't be reduced to a typology or a number. That said, I have found the Enneagram very valuable to better knowing and understanding myself, which helps me lean into the good aspects and seek to mitigate the bad.

# 10:  NOW

The previous nine chapters outlining my past bring me to *now*. I'm writing this last chapter where I began over ten years ago, at Conception Abbey in Conception, MO, in October 2019. I arrived yesterday on a windy but beautiful autumn day, and the first thing I did was walk the campus, visiting the lake, the pond, and of course, the apple orchard.

You may remember from chapter seven that my visit to that apple orchard in April 2007 was a turning point in my spiritual journey, where I felt God speak to me through the buds that were appearing on the pruned branches of the apple trees, giving me hope that *my* pruning was going to result in new life and abundant fruit. As I approached the orchard yesterday, I welled up with emotion at this memory (and well up again as I write this). And as I got closer, I began to see them clearly. Apples. Lots of them. Different varieties, golden, green and red, some well past when they should have been picked, but some still pristine. I picked a red one, rubbed it vigorously on my jeans, and took a bite. By the shape and tartness, I could tell it was a Jonathan, my favorite. Absolutely delicious. As I savored it under the autumn sun, I reflected on my spiritual odyssey and saw the past 15 years of this bumpy voyage pass before my eyes. After all that has transpired, where am I now?

As the '20s begin, I find myself in a pretty good place. I have been blessed beyond imagination. I have a job that I genuinely like (at least most days), am pretty good at (again, at least most days), and earns us a decent income. I have a wonderful family. Both my parents are still living, and are still a delight to be around. My sister Kristi, her husband Jeff, and their three almost-grown children Cameron, Liz and Jaclyn live 15 minutes away, so I have gotten to see them grow up. I have great relationships with all my children – Erin and her husband Ryan, Haley and her husband Sam, and Jordan and his fiancée Jessica – relationships based on openness and trust, and a shared affinity for Americana music, cornhole, five-point pitch, dancing, laughter, good beer, brown liquor, and discussing politics and spirituality. They all live away now, but plan to settle back in Kansas City, and, I hope, begin producing grandchildren soon.

Without a doubt, the most consistent, wonderful blessing of my life is my wife Michelle. I become more madly in love with her every day. She has been an endless source of love, acceptance and encouragement to me since we began dating 40 years ago – and especially during the dark days of my faith deconstruction. I know it was tough on her, but her steadfast support and presence during those times truly made all the difference. She is smart, beautiful, caring, selfless, fun, and even *funny* in her own special way. I literally don't know what I would do without her. She is simply the greatest joy in my life.

In Ekklesia, now 11 years old and counting, I have found my tribe, the people I do life with and want to grow old with. Dan and Lana, Ron and Mary Ann, Dave and Lynn, Wally and Lisa, and Tim and Julie. My people. We talk about very serious issues, share our joys and sorrows with one another, pool our money to make a difference in peoples' lives, and have massive fun together. Most of us are bad dancers (Lynn being the main exception), but that sure doesn't stop us. These people accept me as I am, have been absolutely critical to my spiritual journey, and are simply indispensable in my life.

On most days, I can even feel some appreciation for my evangelical past, the churches and the people, and especially RidgePoint Christian Church. RidgePoint obviously featured prominently in my spiritual journey, especially my deconstruction. In the previous chapters, I tried to be honest about what I experienced and felt while I was a staff member and attendee there, and as such, I may have come off a little hard on RidgePoint at times. And for sure, earlier on I harbored some bitterness. But now, I generally feel that they were just doing their best, like the rest of us. I experienced tremendous grace and support at RidgePoint, from a wide variety of people there, both before and during my deconstruction. But, especially from pastor Brad, an imperfect but very gracious man who gave a non-theologically-educated marketing researcher a chance at professional ministry, and never failed to take time to listen to me with care and concern when I was struggling.

But, in the midst of all the happiness and joy of my life, I still feel the loss of my evangelical faith and community. Recently on the Liturgists podcast, Hillary McBride, a therapist, researcher, speaker and writer who is one of the Liturgists podcast hosts, talked about how people can experience deconstruction in two ways. For some, it feels like *something they choose*, like they finally have agency to decide what they do and don't believe rather than just accepting what has been handed down to them. As such, they feel more exhilaration and freedom than anguish and loss, and may actually *enjoy* it.

But for others, they experience deconstruction as *something that happens to them* without their choosing or consent. As such, they feel like something is being taken from them, resulting in feelings of fear, pain, and loss. The changes they are experiencing to their faith package were uninvited, and are costing them more than they ever imagined and wanted: theological certainty, security, and a community they can belong to and identify with.

My deconstruction was decidedly the latter. I felt like it happened *to* me, not something I chose. Various experiences, feelings, thoughts and information conspired to make me no longer able to believe what I used to believe. But, at the same time, I didn't want to let it go, it's all I knew. This produced great tension, fear and anxiety. It felt like something was being ripped away from me – my community and how I made sense of the world. I've heard some conservative evangelicals say that leaving the evangelical faith and church is somehow taking the *easy* way out, as if it's simply a capitulation to the lures and temptations of the "world." If this is something you have thought, I hope this book has disabused you of that notion, and that it's self-evident by now that it would have been *far* easier for me to just stay put. At the risk of sounding overly dramatic, deconstruction felt to me like *death*, representing the greatest loss of my life so far.

In many ways, I continue to cope with that loss, and probably will always feel it on some level. My deconstruction ultimately cost me a great deal, and I sometimes have sadness and regret. At times I feel ashamed for spending so much of my adult life in a belief system that I have now mostly jettisoned, like I wasted a big part of my life. When that happens, I tend to "numb out" like a typical Nine by drinking too much and watching a bunch of mindless TV.

But, at some point in the process, the journey transformed from utter reeling and survival to an explicit search for freedom. And ultimately, despite the lingering feelings of loss, I have found greater freedom, and have taken agency over my spiritual journey that now is no longer something that *happens to me,* but rather is more something I *choose.* It's not without its ups and down, but they are far less severe than in the past, and it's now something I can truly say I mostly enjoy. And as unimaginable as this would have been in my evangelical days, or even the first few years of my deconstruction, the key to me finding more peace and freedom has been choosing to increasingly embrace mystery and ambiguity. I used to pursue certainty at all cost, but the more I pursued it, the more out of reach it became. Abandoning the quest for certainty, and becoming more comfortable with not knowing, has made all the difference. I've truly found it freeing to not have to have all the answers.

At times I have expressed concern or regret that my faith deconstruction and my seemingly irresistible urge to talk about it have brought others along on a journey that *they* did not choose. I sometimes have felt guilty about leading people in this way, causing them the same pain that I experienced. But while some of my friends have indeed experienced some pain as a result of their evolving faith, I don't sense that any of them have felt the depth of loss that I have. And, many have seemed to be in the enjoy-it camp, experiencing little-to-no anguish in the process, and welcoming it with alacrity. Regardless, many have expressed their gratitude to me for what I have experienced and shared with them, and that they are more fully awake, free and alive today as a result. I must admit, this is deeply gratifying to me, and makes me think it was all worth it, not only for me, but especially for them.

Perhaps you are experiencing your own faith deconstruction. Maybe you are or have been a conservative evangelical, but have begun having serious questions about your faith, and are feeling disconnected from your faith and community and are experiencing feelings of pain and loss as a result. I hope this book has helped you know that you are not alone, and what is happening to you is not something strange or bad. This has happened to millions and millions already, and will continue to happen, maybe more so as the world opens up in the information age, exposing us all to far more points of view than even as recently as 20 years ago.

If this is where you are, I want to make something clear to you (at the risk of offending any conservative evangelicals who have hung around this far): *conservative evangelicals don't own the Christian faith*. Yes, I know they think they do; the insistence and certainty that they are right is part and parcel of conservative evangelicalism. And evangelicals have undoubtedly won the Christian branding war (at least for now), deftly making "Christian" largely synonymous with conservative theology and politics.

But I hope I have shed some light on alternative ways to be a person of spirituality and faith, even the Christian faith. You don't have to be a Biblical literalist to be a Christian. You don't have to subscribe to all the literal historic Christian doctrines to be a Christian. We don't have to let evangelicals exclusively own Christianity. I simply will no longer give them the authority to decide who's "in" and who's "out," for myself or anyone else, and you shouldn't either. (Quite frankly, a group that has gone all-in on Donald Trump is a group that I think has lost its moral authority, and is generally not a group I'm going to seek guidance from, spiritually or otherwise.) I encourage you to press on, and seek out alternatives – Christian or otherwise – that resonate with you and give you life. Go beyond doctrinal and intellectual pursuits, and explore spiritual practices, especially mysticism, meditation and contemplative prayer. Find fellow journey companions, be honest with yourself and others, and above all, seek love, truth and freedom.

*Still Christian, New Kind or Otherwise?*

I'm sure some of you are wondering, based especially on what I wrote in the past couple of chapters, if I still identify as a Christian. First and

148

foremost, I generally no longer feel the need to put a label on my spirituality. But, while I'm more reluctant to do so than in the past, for reasons I've already given, more often than not I do indeed still identify as a Christian. Here's why.

While I no longer believe that Jesus was the literal son of a Supreme Being born to a virgin, I still believe that Jesus was a preeminent example of a human in real union with the divine. While I don't know that every single word or deed attributed to him in the four gospels actually, literally, historically happened as recorded, I still believe that he was a living, breathing person whose life made a rare and lasting impact on our world. I still believe his teachings and actions are unsurpassed in human history as examples of how to live in unity with one another and the divine, embody non-violent resistance, speak truth to power, and include and show compassion for those on the margins, the oppressed, and "the least of these."

I no longer think Christianity is the only way to a full, loving, compassionate, just life. I believe many religions and philosophies can facilitate a life that is fully awake and alive, with awareness of and in union with Ultimate Reality. All religions and philosophies are merely fingers pointing at the moon; the moon is God, ultimate reality, unitive consciousness, enlightenment, or whatever you want to call a life lived in full wholeness and loving awareness of what is.

I like the distinction that Richard Rohr makes in his recent book *The Universal Christ*. Rohr says that Christ is not Jesus's last name, but rather:

> What if Christ is a name for the transcendent within of every "thing" in the universe? What if Christ is a name for the immense spaciousness of all true Love? What if Christ refers to an infinite horizon that pulls us both from within and pulls us forward, too? What if Christ is another name for everything — in its fullness?

If this is true, then Christ is simply a name of something that all religions and philosophies are seeking. Rohr's distinction between Christ and Jesus is...

Christ is a good and simple metaphor for absolute wholeness, incarnation, and the integrity of creation. Jesus is the archetypal human just like us (Hebrews 4:15), who showed us what the Full Human might look like if we could fully live into it (Ephesians 4:12-16).

He goes on to say, very helpfully in my opinion:

While I don't believe Jesus ever doubted his real union with God, Jesus of Nazareth in his lifetime did not normally talk in the divine "I AM" statements, which are found seven times throughout John's Gospel. In the Gospels of Matthew, Mark, and Luke, Jesus almost always calls himself "the Son of the Human" or just "Everyman," using this expression a total of 87 times. But in John's Gospel, dated somewhere between AD 90 and 110, the voice of Christ steps forward to do almost all of the speaking. This helps make sense of some statements that seem out of character coming from Jesus's mouth, like "I am the way, the truth, and the life" (John 14:6) or "Before Abraham ever was, I am" (John 8:58). Jesus of Nazareth would not likely have talked that way, but if these are the words of the Eternal Christ, then "I am the way, the truth, and the life" is a very fair statement that should neither offend nor threaten anyone. After all, Jesus is *not* talking about joining or excluding any group; rather, he is describing *the "Way" by which all humans and religions must allow matter and Spirit to operate as one.*

It is within this understanding and framework that I can remain in the Christian tradition but still affirm the validity of all religions and philosophies that genuinely seek loving awareness and Ultimate Reality. I also largely hang on to my Christian identity because I believe in death and resurrection. Let me explain.

Regardless of what you believe about what was accomplished by Jesus's death, and the historicity of Jesus's resurrection, what I think is undeniable is that Jesus revealed the essential pattern of reality: death and resurrection. You can take that literally if you want, but I think it's more interesting metaphorically. Life is full of ups and downs, loss and gain, despair and delight, failure and success, sorrow and celebration, sadness and happiness, darkness and light, death and life. You can't have one without the other. Loss, failure, sorrow, death... these are inevitable. But life is resilient and stubborn, and so out of death inevitably comes resurrection: new life, new opportunities, new relationships, new joy, new hope.

This is exactly my story, the deconstruction and subsequent rebuilding of my faith and worldview. I am not the same as I was 15 years ago. I went through a sort of death that will stick with me forever. But, I was and continue to be resurrected and made new. Soon enough, I will experience more death and loss, even eventually my own passing from this life into whatever is beyond it. But in this as well, I have confidence – not *certainty*, but *confidence* – that whatever that is will be just fine, just as it should be.

In my meditation closet, I have a candle that I burn during my contemplative practice. The candles I buy are in small glass jars, and no matter how cheap or expensive a candle is, it simply refuses to burn evenly. As it burns down, invariably there is part of the candle wax that remains high on one side. Because I like evenness and symmetry, I have sometimes embarked on candle surgery, taking a knife and removing the excess wax on the one side in hopes that, by starting evenly again, the candle will burn evenly from now on. And of course, it doesn't.

It struck me recently, as I was watching my meditation candle burn, that this candle is a lot like life. I want it burn evenly, but it refuses to do so. It burns as it burns, which is invariably uneven. But the flame continues on, moving and dancing, providing constancy and variety, but always providing at least some light. More and more, I am becoming accepting and content with that, meeting the unevenness of life and each moment within it with Radical Acceptance and "yes, thank you." I increasingly am able to live, move, and be within the loving presence of the divine (Acts 17:28).

I close with the lyrics to a song I wrote a few years back that is aspirational for how I hope to live and look at my life, called "Live Move Be." It's about detecting the divine in all of life, and it's my wish and my prayer for not only me, but for you as well.

> In him we live and move and have our being.
> In him we live and move and have our being.

God beneath me, God beside me,
God above me, God inside me,
God before me, God behind me,
God my all in all.

In him we live and move and have our being.
In him we live and move and have our being.

God in death and life, God in peace and strife,
God in earth and sky, God in baby's cry,
God in hair of gray, God in yesterday,
God among us today.

In him we live and move and have our being.
In him we live and move and have our being.

God in all we see, God in all we hear,
God in all we feel, God in all we fear.
God in all we love, God in all we hate,
God in all that's now, God in all we wait.
God pervading us, and invading us,
God inviting us, reigniting us.
God containing us, and sustaining us,
Rearranging us now.

In him we live and move and have our being.
In him we live and move and have our being.

If God is for us, who can be against us?

So live, move, be.

In God, live, move, be.

# ACKNOWLEDGMENTS

Many heartfelt thanks to...

My parents, Richard and Norma White, who provided a wonderful home to grow up in, and have modeled resilience, stability, and Radical Acceptance of life as it is, with humor and grace.

My children, Erin, Jordan and Haley, who have turned into fully awake, loving, accomplished adults. You have allowed me to not only be a father, but a human, to struggle and enjoy life with you. And, you let indulge my inner child by letting me do "The Kicking Thing."

My cousin and forever best friend Russ. When I first converted to conservative evangelical Christianity in my late teens, I dreamed that I would be a role model for you to emulate, for you to be more like me. As it turned out, it was the other way around. It took me a while to get there, but I want to be more like you. The ease and non-judgmental acceptance that I see in you and Tonia as you live your lives is a role model to me, and is truly more Christian than anything I can think of.

Our Wichita church friends Derek and Kim, Rod and Annette, and Don and Cathy. You all were our first married couple friends. A lot of years have passed since then, but your presence and encouragement in my life as a young adult set a firm foundation for how I would pursue relationships and community for the rest of my life.

Our Dallas church friends Joe and Terri, Steve and Robbi, and Mark and Debbie. You enveloped us into community in our first big move away from our home state. Your love and support were instrumental in setting me on a path of ministry and leadership.

Oakbrook Church, who allowed me my first shot at church leadership, and encouraged me and looked past my many flaws in doing so.

Pastors and leaders of RidgePoint Christian Church. I am forever grateful for your faith in me, and for allowing me to work alongside you all those years. I'm sure I caused some stress and hurt to you during my deconstruction and my family's leaving. Your gracious treatment of me during that time will never be forgotten.

People from RidgePoint and the Gathering who showed me extraordinary patience and grace and listened to me with no judgment during my deconstruction: Randy, Eric, Darren and Brenda, Brian and Linda, Tara, Bruce, and Bob.

Jim, who introduced me to the Mug Club and spiritual director Craig, and has been a gracious, accepting and challenging friend in this journey throughout the years.

Craig from Rhythm of Grace, whose Pilgrim's Process set me on a path to a more holistic and contemplative spirituality, and whose teaching and calming and accepting presence was a huge help and stabilizing force in my life in 2007.

Mug Club original members Dan, Charlie, Lance, Justin, and Tom, and later members Paul, Dave, and Jim. Your acceptance and encouragement of me when I was at my lowest during my deconstruction was life-saving, and conversations we had sitting around a high-top drinking delicious discounted beer were instrumental in my finding joy, peace and freedom again.

My Ekklesia community: Dan and Lana, Ron and Mary Ann, Dave and Lynn, Wally and Lisa, and Tim and Julie, and alumni/members emeritus Phil and Terri and Jim and Ryan. I choose you! Your presence and encouragement are unrivaled in my life. What we have talked about, struggled through, and experienced these past 11 years has largely made me who I am (for good or bad!). Without you I could not have done this.

My wife Michelle: without your listening ear, shoulder to cry on, and constant encouragement, this book most certainly never would have happened. My life is blessed beyond imagination because of you. I love you so much, and can't imagine a more perfect partnership.

And finally, God, and all the names you go by – Ultimate Reality, Spirit, the Divine, etc. You are ultimately the reason for this book. Although I no longer think of you as a supreme being, and sometimes have no idea who, what or even *if* you are, I still often experience you as loving and personal. Thank for you for never leaving me, and still, after everything, being real and present in my life.

# ABOUT THE AUTHOR

Brian White is a former pastor who now does marketing research, and co-leads a theologically-progressive house church in his spare time. He lives in the Kansas City area with his wife Michelle, and has three grown children.

Made in the USA
Coppell, TX
17 November 2020